The Secret World
of
Money

by
Andrew M. Gause

SDL Press
Hilton Head Island, S.C.

First Printing
July 4, 1996

Cover Art
Jill Opperman Graphics

Additional copies
available for purchase
Please send your inquiry to:

Andrew M. Gause
Box 198
Hawthorne, NJ 07507

Phone orders:
973-423-2200

*Dedicated to everyone who
ever told me to write a book*

With special thanks to:
Christopher DuHaime for his brilliant research, to Fred
Dashevsky for holding it all together, and to Gina Pontrelli,
for "impediment elimination". Also, a special thanks to
the professional staff at SDL, without whom this would not
have happened: Matthew, Jennifer, Rick, Donna,
Anthony, Jason, De Dee, Meg, and Susan.

Much has been written about money and, as this book goes onto that pile, I wonder about its impact. I speak to many individuals about these matters and find that limited knowledge abounds. If I can expand one horizon or open one pair of eyes to a subject that touches the lives of all, then I have succeeded in my goal.

A. Gause
July 4, 1996

The Secret World of Money

What is money?

Money, defined simply, is "a medium of exchange". A "medium of exchange" can be said to be anything which serves to facilitate the exchange of things by providing a common basis of measurement. Instead of a farmer trading potatoes for clothing, and then trading the excess clothing for milk, he trades his potatoes for money, which can then directly be traded for milk. Money is used as a trading medium. In its ideal form money represents actual stored human effort.

Is there a "legal" definition for the word "money"?

Black's Law Dictionary defines money as follows: "In usual and ordinary acts it means coins and paper currency used as circulating mediums of exchange, and does not embrace notes, bonds, evidences of debt, or other personal or real property. A medium of exchange authorized or adopted by a domestic or foreign government as its currency."

What items have served as "money"?

Money has taken many forms throughout history. Gourds, stones, feathers, beaver pelts, sticks, bronze axes, and dozens of other items that we might now consider odd choices for currency have served as money. In ancient Greece, oxen were used as the basic unit of exchange. When gold and silver coins were finally introduced into the culture, the ox remained the basis for metal money, with each of the various coins being valued as various fractions of an ox. In the Early days of Rome, Caesar paid his troops with cakes of salt. In fact, the word "salary" comes from the Latin word "sal", meaning salt. When the early American settlers found that clamshells (known as "wampum") were the most useful material they could have for trading with the Indians, they began to use it for trading among themselves. In 1637, the government of Massachusetts made wampum legal tender. While we may consider some of these choices as odd, many were quite successful. One-inch square, notched rods of hazel wood called Tally Sticks (some up to four foot in length) were successfully employed as the basic monetary unit in England from 1100 to 1826.

What is a "Dollar"?

The word "dollar" originally came from the Bohemian word "thal", which meant "valley". A silver coin was minted from the silver found in Joachimsthal, Bohemia (Joachim's Valley). The coin became known as "a thaler", which soon after became translated into English as "a dollar". During the 1700's, the Spanish produced a silver coin almost identical in size and weight to the thaler. Merchants called it the "Spanish Dollar". In 1785, Congress accepted the Spanish Dollar as the official unit of value for the United States and proclaimed that all other coins, foreign and domestic, would be evaluated in terms of the Spanish Dollar. In 1786 the Board of the Treasury officially fixed the silver content of the adopted dollar at 375.64 grains of fine silver. It was subsequently adjusted to 371.25 grains of fine silver. It is important to realize that a "note" for a dollar is not a "dollar". A dollar is a unit of measure, similar to an ounce or quart, and therefore one cannot properly claim that he has a dollar in his pocket, but rather that he has a dollar in silver or a dollar in gold, or "a one dollar note" in his pocket. Per Title 48 Stat 1730, the dollar is fixed at 15 and 5/21 grains of standard gold, and was to be maintained at this level "in perpetuity."

How was the value of a dollar "fixed" at the time of the Constitution?

As prescribed by the Constitution, monetary values were to be fixed in metal and approved by Congress, and any change in the standard was a matter of public record. At the time the Constitution was adopted, the dollar was fixed and defined as 375.64 grains of fine silver. Six years later the Coinage Act was passed, and the dollar was fixed.

What is a "note"?

An instrument containing an express and absolute promise of the signer to pay to a specified person or order, a definite sum of money on demand.

What is meant by the term "currency"?

Coined money and such bank notes or other paper money as are authorized by Law, which do in fact circulate from hand to hand, as a medium of exchange.

What is "legal tender?"

All coins and currency of the United States, including Federal Reserve Notes, and circulating notes of Federal Reserve Banks, and national banking associations, regardless of when issued, are legal tender for all debts, public and private, public charges, taxes, and dues, in the United States.

What are Federal Reserve Notes?

Federal Reserve notes are evidences of debt to a private bank. Their quantity and value are determined by a group of businessmen who own this private bank.

Are Federal Reserve Notes "dollars"?

No. The Federal Reserve wants us to believe that their notes are dollars.

Are Federal Reserve Notes Constitutionally valid as money?

Federal Reserve notes are Legal Tender, but are not in fact Constitutionally lawful money. Per Article 1, Section 10, Clause 1 of the Constitution: "No State shall make any thing but gold and silver coin a tender in payment of debts."

Did Federal Reserve Notes replace money?

A Federal Reserve Note is not in itself, money, but it is a promise to pay money. It is not the payment itself. Imagine if you were able to convince everyone in your town to accept your personal checks for goods and services, and then you additionally convinced them that instead of cashing your checks they should just pass them on to others, who in turn would accept them as payment for goods and services. If you were able to do this, you wouldn't need to have any money in your checking account! Moreover, the amount of checks or "promises to pay" you could write would be virtually without limit. The Federal Reserve bank has no actual "money" in its account to back up the "notes" it writes, so it has, over the years, quietly removed the written promises to pay which used to appear on the face of each of their notes. Federal Reserve notes have replaced money as the circulating medium of exchange.

What are "precious metals"?

Tangible assets can be broken down into two distinct categories. The first is precious metal bullion. The second would be numismatic or semi-numismatic coins. Precious metal bullion can currently be purchased at a specific exchange rate. The problem is that this value is set overseas. The "London fix" is where on a daily basis the price of gold is set per ounce.

What is "inflation?"

Inflation is defined as: "The printing and release of cash receipts which are not backed by acknowledged gold or silver precious metals". This depreciates the value of the printed receipt in relationship to the precious-metal backing, and the amount of printed money in circulation. This is the only real and valid definition of inflation. Generally, inflation can be said to be any increase in the money supply. When a government simply chooses to issue more and more currency to cover increasing obligations as prices rise, inflation can reach impossible levels. From 1986 to 1991 the Peruvian economy experienced an incredible two million percent inflation of their national currency, the "Sol".

Are "higher prices" the same as inflation?

Ever-higher prices are the result of a privileged group introducing into and bidding in the marketplace "Fed-created dollars". Prices rise as a result of this action, but rising prices are not inflation. Inflation is merely the action of increasing the money supply. Rising prices are the result of this inflation.

What is "The Money Supply"?

The amount of money in the economy at any point in time. It consists of funds in circulation, as well as in checking accounts. It has been generally divided into four groups based upon liquidity. The groups are "M-1", "M-2", "M-3", and "L".

What is "M-1"?

"M-1" are funds in circulation - cash money, checking accounts, and drafts.

What is "M-2"?

"M-2" consists of "M-1" as well as all Mutual funds, overnight repurchase agreements, and savings accounts.

What is "M-3"?

"M-3" includes "M-2" as well as long-term purchase agreements and time deposits in excess of $100,000.

What is "L"?

"L" includes "M-3" as well as bankers' acceptances, T-bills, and similar long term investments. "L" is the sum total of all money.

Why should one be interested in the Money Supply?

It's interesting to note the rate at which "L" has been increasing. Looked at as a simple supply and demand equation, if the supply of money determines its price, then the value of money should have fallen by thirty percent in the last five years. The factor that keeps experts guessing is the percentage of money that is in long-term retirement accounts, because that money is not actively competing for goods and services. In 1950 just three percent of the Nation's assets were being held in the form of long-term retirement accounts. Therefore, any change in the money supply was felt instantly at the cash registers. In today's economy, over twenty-five percent of the Nation's wealth is held in these long term-type accounts. This is why inflation is not readily apparent, but yet it is a serious, looming problem. Inflation won't really hit until the owners of that long-term money turn it into current money.

What is "debt money?"

Currency based on evidences of debt. Under the Federal Reserve System, the only way currency enters circulation is through the creation of debt. When any commercial entity, (including you and I), enters a debt contract (i.e. mortgage, credit card), the debt obligation is monetized or exchanged at the Federal Reserve Bank for a similar amount of Federal Reserve notes. All currency in circulation has been borrowed into existence, and must eventually be repaid with interest.

What does the term "Debt" mean?

Legally, it has various meanings; "A sum of money due by certain and express agreement. A specified sum of money owing from one person to another, including, but not only, obligation of debtor to pay, but the right of a creditor to receive and enforce payment liability on a claim. A fixed and certain obligation to pay money or some other valuable thing or things either in the present or in the future. In a still more general sense, that which is due from one person to another, whether goods, services, or money. In a broad sense, any duty to respond to another in money, labor, or service. It may even mean a moral or honorary obligation unenforceable by legal action. Also, sometimes an aggregate of separate debts, or the total sum of the existing claim against a person or a company."

What is the "debt virus"?

The term is used to describe the economic effects of only bringing money into circulation through the issuance of debt. Since the money needed to pay interest is not created when the debt is created, the debt is multiplied, until it eventually engulfs the economic system. Like a virus, the debt multiplies exponentially.

What is "fiat currency"?

Currency not backed by gold or silver. The word "fiat" means "command" or "decree", translated from Latin as "Let it be so". Fiat money derives its legitimacy from the issuer's power to tax, or to punish. When we look at history, we see that every fiat currency has failed. Fiat currency has no real value behind it. As long as "faith and credit" are serviceable, a semblance of order can be maintained. Historically, every attempt to intangibly back currency has failed.

What are United States Notes?

United States Notes are like Federal Reserve Notes, except that they are the direct obligation of the United States. Regardless of their face value, their cost is only 3 cents. The Federal Reserve Bank estimates there are 597 billion dollars outstanding in Federal Reserve Notes. If we replaced these with United States

Notes at a cost of 3 cents each, the initial savings would eliminate the budget deficit for the next three years, and the annual interest savings would exceed 45 billion dollars!

How did the English "Tally System" work?

Tally Sticks were introduced to England by King Henry the First, the fourth son of William the Conqueror. Henry came to the throne in 1100. When King Henry ascended to the thrown, he found that his Treasury was empty. Needing a supply of money, and not having any, he declared that square rods of wood, issued by his Treasury, would serve as the country's official currency. Tally sticks were narrow shafts, normally hazel, but also willow, box, or other seasoned wood, varying in length from eight inches to as long as three feet, flattened with a knife. The sum of money representing the value of the transactions was cut across the stick in notches. Higher denominations were indicated by deep notches on the face of one side of the stick, lower denominations were represented by smaller notches. There was a ten-Pound stick, a twenty-Pound stick, and so on. After the stick had been notched, it was split lengthwise through the notches, with one piece slightly longer than the other, and that piece was "the tally". After slicing it lengthwise, Henry put one-half in his Treasury, and then spent the other half into circulation. When citizens remitted the sticks back as payment for taxes, Henry's Treasury verified the payment's authenticity by matching it with its other half, whereupon the whole stick was retired from circulation. That was really the first large-scale fiat currency system, and it was quite successful for over 600 years. King Henry got credit for that currency system, when in reality the idea for fiat currency went back to the Chinese Emperors.

How did the King convince his English subjects to accept the Tally Sticks?

Henry built demand for the tally stick money by requiring that they be used to pay taxes. It was the sovereign power to levy and collect taxes which instilled this demand for otherwise worthless pieces of wood. They were used exclusively as money in England for 594 years, and partially for 89 years. A six-hundred-year run with the tally stick wasn't bad. That was the golden age of British society, when Britain really had the power.

How did the English use the tally-sticks in day to day commerce?

If someone paid you with the King's tally stick, you paid someone else with the King's tally stick. It was accepted by all those under rule of the King, and eventually whoever owes a duty to the King would obtain and set aside an appropriate quantity of sticks for remittance back to the King for payment of taxes.

Could tally sticks be used outside England?

The sticks had to be used within the realm.

How would the King make purchases out of the country?

He would utilize the services of a banker, usually a Rothschild. His banker would convert his tally sticks into gold currency, charging a discount rate.

Does the Bible make any reference to an ideal money system?

There is no prescribed monetary system in the Bible.

What are "Supernotes"?

There's a tremendous amount of interest in the "Supernote" story. The Treasury is telling us that they have designed and issued the new currency in order to foil attempts at counterfeiting using the latest computerized color laser copy machines. But in the Bekka Valley, there is alleged to be a group of operatives who are printing up perfect US one-hundred-dollar bills with US Treasury printing presses and actual plates. Back in the 1980's, the East German Secret Police had engravers make the plates after the Bureau of Engraving and Printing sold the Shah of Iran a US Treasury printing press. Representative Jim McCollum revealed these facts to the people of the United States during Special Hearings. Not only did we sell the former Shah of Iran the press, but we sent technicians over there to align it and calibrate it for him. When more radical factions seized power, the press fell into the wrong hands. So now, in the Bekka Valley in Lebanon, there is a printing press which prints US currency that the Feds refer to as Supernotes; super-quality counterfeit 100 dollar bills. When the Secret Service and the Federal Reserve Bank can't tell them apart from the real thing, how on earth are you and I supposed to? Most hotels in Europe will not even take a one-hundred dollar bill anymore. Our Treasury claims it will introduce the newly-designed 1996 series bills without removing the old ones from circulation. If the reason that the Treasury is issuing the new hundreds is because the old ones are being counterfeited so well that we can't tell them apart, and if we are willing to trade the old ones for the new ones, aren't we in effect subsidizing that Middle Eastern operation?

What is "the Money Plane?"

In addition to the Supernotes, there's another very curious ongoing situation regarding our currency. Republic National Bank of New York is flying billions of dollars' worth of one-hundred dollar bills over to Russia. There are already over 220 billion dollars in US one-hundred dollar bills circulating in Russia. I think that one day, very soon, the US Treasury will outlaw, or demonetize, the old money in favor of the new. I believe that by doing so they could capture 300 billion dollars in money without firing a shot.

What is The New World mine?

A huge gold mine has been proposed just outside of Yellowstone National Park. It's one of the biggest gold finds in North America. It would bring over 100,000 jobs to that region. You'd have miners making twice as much as the average monthly wage for the state. The mine isn't even in the park It's two miles outside the park. Every pressure has been brought to bear to keep this mine from opening, but when it became clear that no domestic pressure could be brought to bear to keep it from opening, then the Interior Secretary asked UNESCO to declare it a World Heritage Site, meaning, "we the people" no longer have sovereignty over the site. Why? If any gold comes out of that mine after it becomes a World Heritage Site, it will belong to the UN. It's a simple land grab. Whoever owns the rights to that land will be rich beyond their wildest dreams.

Who decides what the value of a dollar will be?

This is my problem with the entire current monetary system. Congress gave away its duty to regulate the value of our currency. We need to give the power back to Congress. This way, if anyone wanted to change the value of the Dollar, they would have to do it on the floor of Congress. They couldn't do it behind closed doors. But the system now in place allows Congress to point to the Federal Reserve and say, in effect, "It's all their fault. We don't have anything to do with it."

Is the US dollar the currency against which all other currencies are valued?

We may refer to "so many Yen to the Dollar", but we always talk about "so many Dollars to the Pound". The British Pound is the "king pin", mostly because of the influence of England in all these transactions. From the beginning, the Bank of England has had its hand in all of this. Certainly the cooperation of the Pound is of the utmost importance. Recently, the cooperation of the Mark and the Yen has gained importance to the Fed. But the Pound Sterling is the first really successful fiat currency.

How is our money created?

Instead of your Government printing cash receipts (which were brought in by taxes paid to the Government and backed fully by precious metals), and then releasing those receipts into society, interest free, the Federal Reserve Act of 1913 established the following: The Department of the Treasury calls up the US Mint and declares that the Federal Reserve has expressed the need for one billion dollars to be printed. Since that money is backed by no precious metals, reduction of the value of printed money already in circulation will occur in relationship to the face value of the new money created. The Bureau of Engraving and Printing prints the money. The Federal Reserve then buys the bills from the United States Mint for 234 dollars per 1000 notes. Next, they deposit this money at face value into their own account. They then purchase US Treasury obligations such as T-Bills, T-Bonds, and T-Notes and pay the money they just received right back to the US Department of Treasury, which spends it into the economy. The Federal Reserve Banks, previously having nothing, now have the full face value of the money printed in their account. Additionally, they will receive the interest which will be paid on this money.

Does our Congress determine the value of our current dollar?

No. The value of American currency is now set behind closed doors by officials of the Federal Reserve Bank.

What's wrong with our current monetary system?

The flaw in the present system is that our Government has been convinced that it is perfectly normal for a Nation to borrow its national currency from (and pay interest to) a private bank, instead of simply issuing whatever amounts of currency it needs directly from its own National Treasury.

Is there an alternative to Federal Reserve Notes?

Yes, there is. Title 31 United States Code, Section 5115 allows the President to issue over 300 million dollars in United States Notes, interest-free, from the Treasury.

Is Congress sufficiently competent to take back control of America's money supply?

Actually, disbanding the Fed and giving back to Congress the power to regulate the money supply would immediately force fiscal prudence upon every Congressman. The Fed now enables Congress to spend our children's and grandchildren's money. The political implications of creating massive amounts of bonded debt are not felt for years. But if Congress did not have the ability to issue bonds, but rather had only the ability to issue currency in the form of US Notes, any extravagant issuance of currency would cause an inflation that would get Congress thrown out instantly. In other words, by being careless with the money supply, Congress would be committing political suicide. That's the way our Forefathers intended it to be. If you're a politician and you're going to authorize the creation of excess money to fund pet projects, then the resultant inflation is going to be felt on your watch.

Is a flat tax better than a graduated income tax?

We will not get anywhere in this country until we stop taxing production and start taxing consumption. The average worker working 40 hours per week might actually bring home less money if he works 45 hours. It's a deplorable situation. A flat tax is no different than a graduated tax. It's still a direct tax. I have a problem with the notion of allowing multi-national corporations to import products into this country tax free, and then taxing the wages and life-blood of the American people. If I decide I'm going to start a garden and grow vegetables so I don't have to pay a tax on them, I want to do it. It would encourage a drop in consumption. We need less consumption. We need more savings. We need more production. We can't be the world's consumer. We can't have other nations producing goods and then bringing them here for us to consume. We need to produce. We have encouraged our corporations and people not to produce. How many farmers are we paying not to grow? The idea of stopping or slowing production in this country is extremely wrong and harmful. We should get off the path of taxing production, and start taxing consumption.

Should the US be more protectionist in its economic policy?

There is a certain amount to be said for that. What little industry remains in this nation should be protected. You cannot manufacture wealth out of thin air. You need a productive society.

How does money come into existence today?

The government (or a quasi-government corporation) issues bonds, and announces that "x" percent will be paid to investors. Let's say that ten billion dollars' worth of bonds are issued. Investors buy three billion dollars and write checks from the existing supply of money. The Fed now has to buy the rest, write a check for seven billion dollars, and give it to whomever issues the bond. The seven billion dollars is created by the Fed. It did not exist before. That is the way money is created, right then and there. In the old days, when the King created money and paid it to the workmen working for him, everyone could look at the money and know it was the King's money. Additionally, when the King issued notes at his prerogative, or when the Massachusetts Bay Colony issued notes, there would have to be a proclamation such as "The Massachusetts Bay Colony is issuing 12 million pounds of currency." With such public announcements, everyone could keep track of the quantity (and therefore the quality) of that money. But now, with the Fed writing the check for seven billion dollars worth of bonds, and commingling it with three billion dollars that legitimate investors paid, there's no way to distinguish the King's money from the real money. That's really the beauty of this Federal Reserve system. It homogenizes the money.

What is meant by "homogenizing the money"?

Prior to 1913, different bank notes were issued by many different banks. Some banks were better than others, and people were more willing to accept the notes of a good bank than notes from a bank with a questionable reputation. The main benefit of the old banking system was that it enabled the citizen to see the difference between bank-created money and real hard-earned lawful money, backed by something. But once the Fed began homogenizing the money supply by blending in real, hard-earned investor money with the Fed's own "created-from-thin-air money", it was impossible to differentiate the true worth of the currency as well as the real extent of inflation.

Who decides when bonds will be issued?

Congress. The way that it's designed, bonds are issued when the Government spends more than it takes in. We recently raised the statutory debt limit. The debt ceiling acts as a pre-approved credit limit. Until they reach that point, Congress can go ahead and write all the checks it wants. Each time a check is written, and there's not enough revenue to cover it, then a bond is issued. The Treasury is authorized to make up the shortfall up to the pre-approved debt limit. Until the recent ceiling hike from 4.9 trillion to 5.5 trillion, we were at the point where all the bonds that could possibly be issued were issued.

How many bonds has the Treasury issued?

Although the statutory limit for bonded debt for the Treasury is presently 5.5 trillion dollars, it is claimed that the Treasury, or persons acting as agents for the Treasury, have in fact issued at least twelve trillion dollars' worth of Treasury bonds and securities! There is one gentleman in Texas who has gone to court over the matter. The story is that he came into possession of some of these bonds, presented them for redemption, and was virtually kidnapped by Federal investigators. He was trying to cash bearer bonds, international CD's drawn on Federal Reserve Banks. It is interesting to note that the individual was not arrested or charged with any type of counterfeiting. The implication is that, prior to Watergate, the "secret shadow government" we learned about during the Iran Contra hearings sold an enormous quantity of bonds to investors and governments around the world, and these instruments are now coming due.   Those following the matter refer to it as "Treasurygate".

When are US Treasury bonds issued?

Bonds are issued often, and the pace of issue is determined both by the Secretary of the Treasury and by the Congress of the United States. The way that it's determined by Congress is through their setting of the maximum limit that the nation can borrow - the so-called "Debt Ceiling". Congress appropriates money for certain public works, and what the Treasury is charged with doing is spreading out debt however it sees fit. The majority of the debt is funded short-term, but a large percentage of it is funded long term. The Treasury issues bonds. Formerly, they auctioned bonds in a blind auction, where you could say how much you'd be willing to loan, and at what rate, and they would simply take the lowest bidders. Lately, they have turned to this Dutch bidding system where they set the price, and you either pass or play. So, they set the price that the bond is going to sell for, and discount it. This means that if the face value of the bond is one thousand dollars, at maturity it will be worth one thousand dollars. Right now, for example, it's discounted to seven-hundred and twenty-five dollars. You buy it, hold it, and at the end of the thirty-year period you cash it in.

What is the difference between T-bonds, T-Bills, and T-notes?

Bonds are ten to thirty years to maturity, bills mature in three or six months, and notes mature from one to 10 years. A bill is sold at a discount from its face, and it matures to its face amount. The discount will be whatever the interest rate is, divided by whatever the period is. If your bill is a three-month T-Bill, for example, and if the interest rate effective annual yield is 5%, then they divide the annual rate by four, discounting that percentage off of the face value, so a thousand dollar three-month T-Bill would end up costing about 988 dollars. In three months you turn it in, and you get a thousand dollars, so effectively you're being paid the interest rates set. With respect to the Treasury Note, the note is sold at its face value, and then pays a specific amount of monthly interest. Treasury Notes are probably more popular than T-Bills and T-Bonds. Put up one thousand dollars, and if the Bill has a 7% annual yield amounting to seventy-dollars per year, that yield is divided by twelve, and you clip your monthly coupon, mail it in, and receive your $5.83. At the end of the term you get your one thousand dollars back. People prefer T-Notes over T-Bills if they need to have a steady monthly income. Aside from that, a Bill is a short term obligation for which there generally is no secondary market. A Bond is an evidence of debt, promising to pay a specified amount of interest for a specified amount of time, and additionally a promise to pay off the loan on the expiration date. One difference between a Bill and a Bond is that a Bill is instantly good. Bonds are bought at a discount from the face value, but the strips attached to the Bond give it its income. The coupons that are on the big bond are just like the notes. They can package them, strip them, sell the coupons to the investor who needs income, and then sell the maturing part of the bond to the investor who needs the capital growth. Brokers cut the strips off the bottom of the bonds, then sell them separately. As an example of how the coupons are worded, I have a Civil War Bond, and the little coupons on it read, "The State of North Carolina will pay to the Bearer, at the Treasurer's office in the city of Raleigh, on the First day of September, 1864, forty dollars on bond #3223 for one thousand dollars". The body of the bond itself reads, "This hereby certifies that the State of North Carolina justly owes the bearer one thousand dollars, redeemable in good and lawful money in the Confederate States and the Office of the Treasurer of the State of North Carolina, city of Raleigh, on the First day of March, 1882 with interest thereon at the rate of eight percent per annum, payable half-yearly at the said office on the First days of March and September of each year from the Date on this Bond, and until the Principal be paid on surrendering the proper Coupons here under an Act. Witness whereof, the Governor of the said State, in virtue of power conferred by law, has signed this bond."

When a foreign investor buys a US Treasury Bond, is the Bond then shipped to him with the coupons on them?

Yes, but usually his fiscal agent here in the states handles that for him. The interest we're paying on the National Debt is being paid directly to the Bond holders or their agents. The bond holders clip the coupons, and mail them in, and the US Treasury pays out the interest to the bond holders.

Who are the holders of US Treasury Bonds?

They're the individual buying public, the Federal Reserve banks, and other commercial banks. Any time you see the Fed adding liquidity to the money supply, that's how they do it. They buy Bonds. No, they are under no obligation to announce when or how much they are buying.

Where are the world's major Central Banks?

The nine industrialized nations each have their own Central Bank. There is the Federal Reserve Bank of New York, which for all intents and purposes is the central bank of the United States, the Bundesbank of Germany, the Bank of Japan, the Bank of England, the Bank of Canada, the Bank of France, the Bank of Italy, the Bank of the Netherlands, and the Bank of Switzerland.

Should the ideal form of currency represent only finished products, goods, or services?

That's not the ideal form for a money supply. Currency should also be able to represent "future" work. The ability to represent potential wealth not yet produced is the true function of an elastic form of money. "Elastic" expresses the idea that the currency represents unaccomplished production. A promise to deliver future work is just as valid a backing for currency as is work already accomplished. People should be able to bond together in a common cause and issue some form of elastic currency to pay for work and projects that need to be undertaken. A society using currency of this type would find it replaces the need to tax the existing money supply for public projects. By issuing "money certificates" for desirable public programs, citizens would be free from general taxation, but when they were presented with one of these special notes, they would be bound to accept it. That's their contribution to an elastic money system.

Why would an elastic system of currency replace the present system of taxation?

For example, if we wanted to build a road from New York to Tampa, and its cost was ten billion dollars, we would print two billion pieces of paper with "Five Dollars" stamped upon each one, and we would pay those connected to the project with them. They, in turn, would pay them out to their creditors in the region. We would require every citizen to accept these notes, and would allow the holders of these notes to remit them to the Treasury in the form of taxes. The money supply would expand only to the extent needed to accomplish building the road. In the case of a worthy public works project, the citizens would find that the completed project could actually generate ongoing revenues for the Treasury, long after all the notes issued for the project had been retired.

How would a temporary increase in the money supply for worthy public projects bring more revenue to the Treasury?

Let's say we specifically issue currency to get a dam built. The Hoover Dam, for example, was a very worthy project, and it's still producing electricity today, which it sells to surrounding municipalities. Let's say we would have issued temporary "Hoover Dam Notes" for its construction, paid them out to the workers and contractors during construction, then recalled those notes over a number of years in the form of special dam taxes. We would be left with a completely paid-for, income-generating public utility, which would in turn generate perpetual income for the State's Treasury. If a State or government were to fund a number of worthwhile projects in this manner, the need for general taxation would be nil. In fact, the Treasury would soon face the problem of what to do with surplus revenues!

What types of projects should be financed through the issuance of "special project" currency?

Every State has one or more turnpikes, bridges, or tollways. The George Washington Bridge linking New York and New Jersey is a classic example. It generates cash "hand-over-fist". It was a huge, wasted money-making opportunity for the region. Instead of letting the citizens financially benefit from its construction, it was thrown into the money market for financing, where the bonds were heavily discounted for the benefit of bankers and brokerage houses. A better solution would have been for the state to issue a billion or two "George Washington Bridge Notes", paying them in salaries to the bridge's architects, contractors and workers, then accept the Bridge Notes back in payment of bridge tolls. In a few years, after all the special notes had been paid back in as tolls, the state's Treasury would start to see an enormous revenue stream.

What function do banks serve in an ideal monetary system?

In theory, the local bank serves its community by issuing money to the local businesses and citizens in order to sustain the local economy. Banks began to neglect their role and responsibilities when they discovered it was more profitable to invest in real estate and securities markets. They became profit-motivated and moved away from the concept of servicing the people in their areas. But ultimately, the function of creating money for the area should not be in the hands of private banks, but in the hands of the people themselves. The function should really belong to the Town Council. The Council would vote on which projects are for the common good of the town, then authorize its Treasury to issue the funds needed to accomplish those projects. The Community is either going to thrive or perish based on the quality and content of its citizens. If you have educated, active citizens who are willing to initiate programs for the public good, like building a municipal water system so the town wouldn't have to buy water from a big city forty miles away, then you'd see thriving cities and communities all across America. How would the town finance its own water system? They'd get together and determine that the project was going to cost twenty million dollars, and the Town Council would then authorize the Treasurer to issue twenty million "Town Council Notes". The people of the town would either accept those notes for their goods and services, or they wouldn't. It's all up to them. And that's the way it should be. They determine whether their little community succeeds or not. That's a transfer of power. It moves the power right down to the local level in a hurry... in a heartbeat.

What problems can arise if communities start issuing their own notes?

Localized issuance of currency solves far more problems than it creates. Unpopular or unnecessary projects would become immediately apparent. The repercussions for imprudence would be severe and immediate. Councils that issue more currency than the citizens can tolerate would find local inflation running wild, especially when measured against the standard of lawful money, an ounce of gold or a dollar in silver. It would be the public's own willingness to participate in their local government's financial decisions, and their ability to remove irresponsible officials that would keep local monetary policies honest and sane.

Out of all the monetary systems throughout American history, which one provided the greatest economic stability?

The Sub Treasury System of the 1840's provided America with a solid currency, and enabled Americans to create and experience the greatest period of economic growth in the history of the world. The twenty-year span from 1840 to 1860 is regarded by monetary historians as America's golden age.

What were the events leading up to "America's golden monetary age"?

To really understand why the 1840 boom came about, we have to understand America's prior banking history. In 1791, a twenty-year charter was granted to the First Bank of the United States, which in effect, became the Central bank of the nation. This privately owned bank quickly grew in power and stature through its ability to create paper money and credit. By 1812, this bank and its owners had snatched up many of the critical American industries, and the people urged Congress not to renew its charter. The war of 1812, to my mind, was waged by the British Banking families over the First Bank's cancelled charter. In 1816, as a likely condition for ending hostilities with the British, Congress agreed to issue a new twenty-year charter, creating The Second Bank of the United States. When this second charter was nearing its expiration, President Andrew Jackson became the leading voice in opposing its renewal. Jackson said to the bankers, "By God, you are a den of vipers and I will rout you out!" And that's just what he did. It was Jackson's abolition of the privately-owned United States central bank system that allowed the US to experience a revitalization of economic activity.

What was the Central Bank's reaction to losing its charter?

During the 1830's, Nicholas Biddle, the Second Bank's president, and Andrew Jackson had some very ferocious battles. Jackson refused to deposit any funds belonging to the National Government into Biddle's bank. In retribution, through his agencies in Europe, and through his control of the New York money markets, Biddle orchestrated a severe credit tightening that triggered one of the worst depressions the country had ever known. It was called the Panic of 1837. Interestingly enough, Biddle was later proven to be an agent of the same European banking families who formed the Federal Reserve in 1913.

How did Jackson's banking system differ from the central bank system?

Under Jackson, the concept of a central bank disappeared.

Instead, we had a Treasury that issued subsidiary coinage. It issued coinage directly from the bank. It was the only honest money in circulation. Everything had to be denominated in it, so that you knew, as a merchant, what the hell you were getting! If bankers issued notes, the notes had to be denominated in these dollars, and paid on demand. You didn't have a central monopoly agency issuing currency that was in private hands. So, by having good, honest, solid money, it pretty much kept the bankers in check.

When did Jackson begin to dismantle the central bank?

The war really started in 1832, during Jackson's re-election campaign, when he told the American people, "If you elect me, I'm going to get rid of the bank. If you want to keep the bank, don't elect me. It's your decision." That was his virtual platform for the entire campaign. By re-electing Jackson, the people spoke and said, "We don't want them". But by the end of Jackson's term, Biddle was claiming victory. There were quotations from newspapers of the time in which Biddle bragged that he had won the battle with Jackson; that he had trounced the Administration by exerting his control over note issue. When Biddle's agencies and partners began withdrawing their paper, Americans found that there wasn't enough gold and silver coin in circulation to pay their debts. Mortgages were foreclosed. It was a classic staged depression. And they knew who did it! By going too far, Biddle drove the electorate to Jackson.

How did Jackson finally create a booming economic climate?

Jackson issued good, hard, sound money, and shunned unbacked paper currency. He ensured that no private central bank was allowed to create American currency. Jackson converted the US Treasury into the nation's central bank. It should be noted that his actions resulted in a debt-free Treasury. In fact, there was a surplus. Under Jackson, money flourished. He resumed coinage of silver dollars and minor, subsidiary coins, so that people were once again free to conduct their commerce using something other than paper notes that a private bank controlled.

How long did the Jackson-created period of economic stability last?

1840 to 1861. It was a splendid period in the Nation - a truly great period. I'd like to have been alive then. All Americans were Sovereign Citizens of the Republic. Indeed, this was the finest era in the history of American money.

What ended the success of this system?

The need to finance the Civil War. In 1863, Abraham Lincoln issued "Greenbacks", an unbacked monetary system, via the National Banking Act.

What happened to Lincoln's Greenbacks?

Lincoln was assassinated. Although the National Banking Act remained in effect, the Federal Government didn't exercise its prerogative to issue more Greenbacks.

Assuming we will never return to the gold standard and monetary policy of the 1840's, what monetary system could be put in place to help America regain her economic footing?

In our current system, the US Treasury issues a bond for 10 thousand dollars, gives it to the Federal Reserve, and the Federal Reserve prints up ten thousand notes. The ideal system would be for the Treasury to directly issue the notes. Like Thomas Jefferson said, "if a nation can issue a dollar bond, it can issue a dollar note. The thing that makes the bond good also makes the note good." In an ideal monetary system, this is how it should work: For instance, Congress decides that the people need a road from Maine to Miami, and estimates that road will cost two billion dollars. Congress orders the Bureau of Printing and Engraving to print two billion dollars (at a cost of a few hundred bucks), and then it circulates this money by using the newly printed bills to pay for the road's construction. When the road is finished, Congress demands them back in payment of taxes, or offers a discounted tax rate for people who pay taxes with these notes. The Treasury will eventually get back all the bills put in circulation. There is no inflation with such a system.

What methods of money creation are available to Government?

We have two possible systems of money creation. The first is the public system, called the "Treasury money system". The other is the private system - currently, the Federal Reserve System.

How does the Treasury money system work?

Under the Treasury money system, the Treasury creates the money. This is the way United States Notes were made. Under this system, when the Congress spends money it doesn't have, the Treasury simply creates the money and spends it. Under this public money system, it is up to the Treasury to either collect the money it needs in taxation, or to create the money and spend it into circulation. There is no borrowing involved. Under the public system, the only way unbacked money gets into circulation is when the Federal Government spends it. Under this system, gold and silver could be taken by private citizens into the Mint, and be coined into real money.

How does the Debt Money System work?

Under the debt money system currently in use, the Federal Reserve creates the money and loans it to the Congress, who provides the Fed with Treasury bonds as collateral for the loan. In our current system, the only way money gets into circulation is when we enter into a commercial obligation with a bank, and the bank creates it.

Does use of the Public Treasury money system require gold backing for the currency?

<u>No</u>. One of the things I want to stress is that I'm not a "gold standard" advocate. I'm a "standard Dollar" advocate. There's a big difference. I don't suggest that the US Government has to own an ounce of gold for every twenty Dollars that it issues. I just suggest that the Dollar be of a standard unit of measure. If the Dollar is officially determined to be twenty to an ounce of gold, it doesn't matter if they have the ounce of gold or not, as long as they understand that there are only twenty to an ounce of gold for a "standard dollar".

Under the Public Treasury money system, how does the Treasury know how much currency to create and place into circulation?

The amount is based on appropriations by Congress.

Would the Treasury have to be concerned about matching the money supply to the Nation's production level?

No. Congress would, though.

Are Congressional appropriations currently linked to what the Country is doing as a producing entity?

No, and that's the point. They really don't care. They currently appropriate and spend regardless of what the Country's needs, and that's very harmful for those of us trying to earn a living under the current system.

Under the Treasury money system, how would Congress gauge how much money to appropriate and spend?

The answer is "re-election"... it's just that simple. The way that our system is supposed to operate is for all appropriation bills to originate in the House. The House of Representatives is up for election every other year. Under the Treasury money system, if Congress appropriated seven billion dollars to build a monument to The Canadian Speckled Goose, they'd either have to immediately raise taxes, or the Treasury would have to create seven billion dollars and spend it into the economy. If they raised taxes for that project, the people would revolt. And if the Treasury created seven-billion dollars and spent it into circulation for that project, the people would also revolt. Either way, the Congressmen who voted for that project are not going to get re-elected. However, under the current system, Congress is free to appropriate money for all sorts of outlandish projects. Why? Because the Treasury is able to quietly take a 30-year loan from the Fed and avoid the wrath of the voters and taxpayers. The only taxpayers who are going to complain are the ones who, in thirty years, will be faced with paying the bill. The public treasury money system is the answer to this dilemma.

Is the Treasury Money System practical during times when production has to be stimulated, such as in wartime?

In the case of creating truckloads of currency to fuel a wartime economy, the Congress needs to have the people solidly behind them. If the people aren't behind the leaders urging them to war, then they're not going to sacrifice. If they're not going to sacrifice, Congress is not going to be successful in funding that particular war. So it had better be a popular war. For example, war could not be justified simply because J.P. Morgan is owed 1.7 billion dollars and if the US doesn't enter the war, then Britain will go under, and Morgan will lose 1.7 billion dollars. That's not a good reason to go to war. Under the system that our Forefathers handed us, we wouldn't go to war for J.P. Morgan. I think the Founding Fathers knew that at some point down the line, those in control of our military would use it to enforce collection of private debts. By prohibiting Congress from borrowing war money from private banks, the Public Treasury System helps to ensure such wars cannot be fought.

Is the Public Treasury system in operation anywhere today?

Yes. In Guernsey. It's part of the Channel Islands of Great Britain. It's where those famous cows come from. Their money is denominated in Pounds, drawn by the States of Guernsey. Their public treasury system started right after the Napoleonic

Wars, around 1820. Legend has it that the islanders needed a local covered market at the port in order to sell their cows. The islanders did not want to borrow the money, so they issued their own notes. They printed up the notes and spent them for the market's construction. When the covered market was completed, they rented out stalls, accepting the Guernsey notes back as payment for stall rental. Every time they took in a Guernsey note, they would burn it. Within ten years, the notes were all burned, there was no interest paid to banks, and the building continued to generate income for the island government. The building is still there, to this day.

Do the inhabitants of Guernsey still use these notes?

Yes. They issue their notes for many other programs. The island operates exactly under the Public Treasury credit money system.

Under the Guernsey system, as the notes are withdrawn from circulation, are there recessionary cycles created as the money supply dwindles?

Not really. The money that was used to build the market was created debt free. And unless such money swamps the existing supply of money, (and remember we are talking about an expenditure of ten thousand dollars in an economy that generated 500,000 dollars), it's really a small increase. The monetary needs of a Federal Government should be limited. The US Government is not supposed to be an all powerful source of unlimited funding, needing billions and billions of dollars in order to operate. It's just not the way the Federal Government was intended to operate. When a Federal Government needs so much money that by creating it they cause inflation and by destroying it they cause deflation, they have exceeded their bounds, and the government officials responsible should not be re-elected. Elected officials are supposed to be thinking about this when they are appropriating money and spending it. They should always be asking themselves, "What's the immediate economic impact here?"

What are some other examples of the Public Treasury Money System in operation today?

Just look at the US Post Office and their stamps. They issue and cancel stamps by the ton every day. They issue the stamp, they cancel it, and they deliver the letter. They create their "money" and they extinguish their "money".

Are Guernsey notes backed by precious metal?

When the Guernsey notes were originally issued, a Pound Sterling was a known quantity of silver. The silver backing has since been withdrawn. Guernsey is on the same fiat standard we are, but they have a way of measuring what their monetary needs are based on the British Pound. The Pound is still the standard.

As a hypothetical case, how would a group of ten individuals use the Public Treasury system to serve their group's economic needs?

Imagine an island on which ten people reside. There are ten gold coins on the island, and everyone needs one gold coin to live. Let's say ten residents get together and decide they want to build a church. The church is going to cost ten gold coins to build, but the residents don't want to take the ten gold coins out of circulation, as everyone will starve while the church is being built. Instead, they can issue ten "gold coin notes", and decide that everyone will pay one gold coin's worth of currency during the coming year for the use of the church. The island treasurer scribbles out ten gold coin notes, and pays out those notes to everyone building the church. When the church is built, the notes are accepted back each Sunday by the church as a "churchgoers' tax". In one year, the church is paid for, and the tax can be abolished. In this example, the island money supply was temporarily increased, the church was erected, the notes were withdrawn, and no one's standard of living was adversely affected.

What are some other benefits of using the Public Treasury money system?

Another important feature is that whoever uses the benefit, pays for it. For example, the Government can build a road from D.C. to Maryland for the commuters, and levy a tax only on the commuters who use the road. If the road costs 100 million dollars, the Congress can authorize the Treasury to issue 100 million US Notes to pay for the road construction. When the road is completed, they can apportion the cost of the road directly to the commuters by charging a one dollar toll. After the road is used 100 million times, it's paid for, and the people can decide whether to keep the toll in place to generate additional revenue for the region, or to cancel the toll charge entirely.

Is that how several states paid for construction of their own Interstate Tollway Systems?

No. That is what we were told, but that is not the reality of what occurred and what continues to occur. In reality what happened was that the Government set up a corporation like the New Jersey Turnpike Authority, a quasi-public organization that issued bonds backed by the State, and then used the revenues as it chose to... not necessarily to reduce the debt of the road. The classic example is the Garden State Arts Center. This huge arts and exposition center was built with the funds they collected from the Parkway. They gave the Arts Center Director a seven hundred thousand dollar salary, then gave the board a few limos, but they didn't do what they were supposed to do with the money. Another example is the George Washington Bridge. It's been paid for 800 times since it opened. That's a lot of times.
Now it's being used purely as a revenue source.

Is there anything wrong with the Government undertaking projects that service the citizens and collect revenue?

Not necessarily. As long as they use that revenue to reduce our taxes, and don't give control of it over to a private authority.

Don't take every single profit-generating operation that this country owns, from the Hoover Dam to the George Washington Bridge, convert their titles to a private authority, then allow the directors of that authority to assume absolute jurisdiction over the asset. We've got the Port Authority of New York and New Jersey with directors earning six-figure salaries flying around in helicopters and riding around in limos, and it's not right.

How are the board members and directors of the various "State Authorities" chosen?

They are all appointed by the various Governors as payback for campaign backing. In my own State of New Jersey, we can find many examples. We have the New Jersey Sports Authority, New Jersey Turnpike Authority, Garden State Parkway Authority, Port Authority of New York and New Jersey, and it goes on and on. All of them are private corporations, with boards of directors and employees and CEOs, and each position is loaded with perks. A paper recently did a blistering expose on what these people are taking out of the Turnpike, and it's shocking.

Are there Federal "Authorities"?

On the Federal level, consider the Tennessee Valley Authority. Do you know how much energy that entity produces? It's mind boggling. Take a look at the list of directors and high paid executives of the TVA. It reads like the Administration's Campaign Contributors list. Every four years it shifts. Every time the Administration in Washington changes, everybody in the TVA is fired and new people come in. The TVA was the first authority to be created. The big players learned how to take money out of the system through the TVA, and it was all downhill from there. With these authorities, there's no Congressional appropriation of funds. The authorities generate tax revenue, but it's not going into the Treasury, so it doesn't have to be taken out of the Treasury in public view. It can be taken out the back door by the truckload. The taxpayers are subsidizing these huge payoffs. In the case of the TVA, they charge for the energy. In the case of the Tunnel and Turnpike Authority, they charge tolls. In the case of the Port Authority, they charge port fees, entry fees, and airport fees. These are all hidden costs for the taxpayers, but the various Authorities don't have to submit to public accountings of money taken in.

Do the Authorities ever remit portions of their revenues back into the State or Federal Treasuries?

Never. The various Treasuries never see a dollar of it. Congress appropriates no funds to the Authorities, so Congress really has no control over them. The Turnpike generates its own money, so it doesn't have to go to the Legislature each year and ask for appropriations, and therefore it's not under Congressional authority. It's the same with the George Washington Bridge. The TVA also doesn't need to apply to Congress for operating expenses. The Hoover Dam doesn't, either. These activities continually throw up huge streams of income, but that income is somehow always sucked back up by salaries and operating costs.

Were the Authorities initially funded by bond issues?

Yes. The Government backed the bond issues. When the operations were up and running and when the Government-guaranteed bonds were retired, these agencies were left to generate income and do with it as they saw fit. This idea was born in the 1930's. The Administration wasn't looking for competent entrepreneurs. These ventures were established as political payoffs. All these projects were established by Executive Orders. The WPA, FTC, FAA, FDA, Agriculture Department - all of them were born by Executive Orders issued under the newly expanded Federal Jurisdiction. The same thing that makes Federal Reserve Notes good makes all of these organizations good. The Federal Government has no Constitutional jurisdiction over water, power, or toll roads between states. It assumed that jurisdiction under Admiralty law. That's why it's so important to study this, for they're all deviations from a lawful, open, Public Treasury system.

In the case of municipal projects, what role did Andrew Jackson's Public Treasury system have?

Individual bond issues were floated in the money markets for whatever project had to be done. If someone thought it was a good idea to connect the Great Lakes to the Railroad, they would issue bonds in a public marketplace, and make it either a private activity, or a for-profit activity, and go at it. If something was viable, then it got done. There are modern-day examples of worthwhile projects attracting money, such as the Chesapeake Bay Bridge Tunnel. If something is necessary, and clearly makes sense, there is never a problem raising the funds to do it. You fund it through bonding, and people with money buy the bonds. When we say bonds, we mean privately-issued bonds or municipal bonds, whichever is appropriate. If it's something like a municipal water supply, then the municipality could issue a bond or a "tax anticipation note". It's effectively the same thing. It's a way to create money without creating money. Let's assume the people of the United States are convinced that we need a given project. The bond would then be issued in the name of that project or Authority, and brought to the marketplace through an underwriter.

Who makes the determination that a public project will require bonds to be issued?

That's what they teach in economics school as the accepted method of finance. Every City Treasurer on the planet knows that. That's the way they've been taught to finance municipal undertakings. They go to an underwriter. The underwriter buys the entire bond issue at a discount, and then distributes it.

What institutions act as underwriters?

Salomon Brothers, Goldman Sachs, Morgan Guaranty, to name a few. Underwriters cannot be banks. That's what the Glass-Steagall Act (also known as the Banking Act of 1933) was all about. The Act made financial institutions separate the functions of banking and underwriting into investment banking and commercial banking. That's what we have today. Yet we're currently seeing incredible banking consolidation. Soon the city treasurers will have their own little commercial branch banker right in their offices. They will be able to bring their issues to market without leaving their buildings. As easily as you and I would call up our bank to acquire a line of credit, that's how easily issues will be underwritten.

What kinds of municipal issues are commonly underwritten?

Water works. Road resurfacing. Capital projects. Things that aren't funded from the immediate Treasury. The types of things that are supposed to generate real wealth.

Whom do the underwriters sell the bonds to?

To institutional investors. In this case, the banks themselves. The Federal Reserve. If an underwriter has a project that no one wants to buy and that everyone figures is a failure, that bond's value is going to erode. There's a danger that it's going to default, and institutions just stay away. They don't buy. Also, if the premium on the money isn't enough, they don't buy. They leave it alone. As a bank, you can buy as much as you want, or as little as you want. The Federal Reserve can buy it all and call it reserves.

Does the Fed buy or own Municipal Bonds?

Here's the official line from the Federal Reserve, and I'll quote it: "The Federal Reserve does not buy or sell gold." That's technically true, I guess. The Federal Reserve system may not buy anything, but the Federal Reserve Bank of New York surely buys and sells gold, and it buys and sells Treasury bonds, and it buys and sells foreign securities, and it buys and sells Telmex. It buys whatever it wants to buy or sell, because it has that authority. It has complete autonomy in that regard through the Federal Reserve Open Market Committee. They will tell you that "No, officially, the Fed does not buy or sell municipal bonds". The reality is that the Fed can buy and sell whatever it wants, and they do it through the Federal Open Market Committee and the Federal Reserve Bank of New York.

Let's say the Government comes up with a plan to build a housing project for "impoverished Americans". Is that a general revenue funds project?

No. Most likely, that will be quasi-public, just like the Turnpike Authority. Imagine this: They would set up the "Government Housing Authority". And the GHA, with the full faith and credit of the United States, would be able to issue 50 million in bonds or "Revenue Anticipation Notes". It's one hell of a scam. The bond issue would generate the 50 million dollars, and, of course, the President would appoint a few of his wealthy campaign financiers as the director and assistant directors, and they all would become even more wealthy.

Are there many such specious special revenue projects?

There are many, many bonds with Government underwriting and Government backing in one form or another. There are so many different types, you couldn't name them all. The originators understand that if they offer a Federal project, the project is as good as gold. The money might as well be gold. It's a guaranteed, insured investment, no question about it. An underwriter takes the whole issue because the Government backs it up. These bonds are slam dunk investments for banks and pension administrators.

Considering the true rate of inflation, why do most pension administrators flock to low yield Government issues?

If you're the administrator of a pension fund, your actuary will tell you that at the officially projected rate of 2.6 percent inflation, the average retiree is going to need only one thousand dollars each month to retire in 2005. That's according to your own actuary. So you follow right along with that line of thinking. As a pension planner, you buy the type of investment that is going to generate those precise numbers. Those numbers are all you care about. If you do better than that, you're a hero. So these people buy municipal bonds, and they don't even have to think about it.

When a municipal bond is sold, what does the money flow look like?

In the case of the Pension fund, the city issues 50 million dollars in bonds through an underwriter. The underwriter book-entries the bond to the pension fund, and then forwards the 50 million dollars minus the underwriting fees to the Treasurer of the town.

Does this action create new money?

It takes existing ledger entries and transfers them. The only entity that has the power to create new money is the partnership between the Federal Government and the Federal Reserve. In the case of government securities, it's up to the Fed to decide whether the administrator can use those securities to create fresh money. We saw an example of this in the Orange County episode, where the County Treasurer took pension funds and leveraged them, thereby creating additional money. He pledged the bonds in the pension fund as collateral for a loan to buy more bonds. He was able to go out ten to one, which of course increased his "reserves" ten to one. So with one hundred million in the Treasury, he was able to get a billion dollars with which to buy securities, in this case, Treasury Bond futures, as he was convinced that interest rates were going down. He guessed wrong, and they lost all their principal premium. In addition, they're liable for the excess loss. It put them in the hole over a billion, I think. Now they have to increase taxes and reduce services.

Is there enough money in most large corporate pension funds to cover their obligations?

The joke is that now the large corporations are saying there's <u>too</u> <u>much</u> money in their pension funds. There's a bill in both the House and Senate. The House Bill will allow private companies to go into their pension funds and take up to 30 billion dollars of that money and spend it, based on the assumption that we only have 2.6 percent inflation, which is the same assumption that the Administration is using. The big corporations and municipalities are saying to Washington, "If you use a 2.6 percent inflation rate to factor your budget, then we get to use that 2.6 rate to factor our pensions." It's incestuous. The numbers being passed back and forth are going to get everyone in trouble eventually.

Ideally, how should needful public projects be financed?

They should be either financed through direct taxation or through the direct issue of bonds.

What is the "crowding-out" effect?

When you go into the economy and you issue a bond to build a railroad which will cost one-third of all of the money in existence, you're pretty much going to put a stop to the rest of human enterprise. Until that railroad is built, and that money has worked its way back into the system, there is no money with which to conduct other commerce. Most of the nation's labor and material resources would flow to that area. That's the "crowding-out" effect everyone talks about. Therefore, if the bond issue is too large, it "crowds-out". People lose their jobs, and politicians don't get re-elected.

Can control be exerted on the Government through deciding which bond issues are brought to the market?

Near the turn of the 20th Century, we had twelve families controlling 80-90% of the wealth of the nation, including capitalizing governments, municipalities and various projects. They were the ones who decided which bond issues were brought to market and which were not. And the projects which were necessarily couched in secrecy were run through as part of general expenditures.

How did gold and silver win out over all the other mediums of exchange used throughout history?

Because of their readily acknowledged beauty, their divisibility, and their relative portability, gold and silver possessed the intrinsic values which met the requirements of most societies for their medium of exchange. Moreover, they were quite scarce and difficult to mine, and no one person controlled their supply.

Why did gold and silver give way to paper as the primary medium of exchange?

Gold and silver can be quite bulky, especially in large quantities. And carting all that metal around can be quite a pain in the neck, not to mention dangerous. Eventually it was determined that something was necessary to represent the gold and silver. It was the weight of gold and silver coins that caused Levi Strauss to put the first rivets on the pockets of his jeans.

How did the use of gold and silver currency help guarantee the rights and political independence of nations?

With a precious-metal backed currency, there exists an absence of complete control by any one person or group. That is a critical component for establishing an ideal currency. Whoever owns, or has total control over, a nation's money supply is the de facto ruler of that nation, no matter the existing form of government. No one person or organization has control over the medium of gold. The gold miner, with his pick axe, has just as good a chance of finding a deposit as a corporation. But in the case of a single Central bank which issues its own private notes as currency, there exists no "competing sources" for the commodity. There is only absolute monopoly and control. I recently asked a State Representative, "What would happen if you issued 'Salt Lake City Notes'? Let's say that Utah wants to build a road from the northern part of Utah to the southern part. What would happen if you introduced a bill on the floor to issue 'Utah Notes' for the project?" He replied that they wouldn't let him do it. Of course not. Utah couldn't issue its own money, even though the legislature could make it perfectly acceptable in payment for all state taxes. So my question to him was this: why should the Federal Reserve Bank, a private corporation owned by wealthy foreigners, run by un-elected officials, and operated behind closed doors, be allowed to do what a Sovereign State cannot do? By what reasoning should they have a monopoly over money creation? Under the current money monopoly system, there is no "competitive miner" who may dig a quantity of money out of the ground and thereby create a certain portion of wealth. A similar monopoly exists in the diamond industry. That industry is strictly controlled by the De Beers corporation. They essentially control the amount of their "currency" out in the market at any one time, and they're doing an admirable job. They understand the nature of their market. Furthermore, they strictly regulate it in typical monopoly fashion. Theoretically, if diamonds possessed the characteristics of money a little more precisely, then De Beers would effectively rule the world.

Is our current money backed by any gold?

In time, "fractional reserve banking" evolved into "zero reserve banking". Under the current Federal Reserve System, your money is not backed by any precious metal at all.

What happened to all the US gold?

All the precious metals which used to be in the reserves of the United States are now stored in underground vaults five floors under the Federal Reserve Bank of New York. This gold has been taken from the American people by the operation of the Federal Reserve Banking system.

How much gold "backs" our money?

Contrary to popular belief, there is not one ounce of gold backing the currency that the Federal Reserve Bank issues.

What backs our currency?

Only the Government's power of taxation lends any value to Federal Reserve Notes.

Where is America's gold stored?

Again, it's not our gold. The largest supply of gold on the planet is buried beneath the former Sub Treasury building, which is now the Federal Reserve Bank of New York. In its vaults is hidden the biggest store of gold on the planet. There is gold in Fort Knox, but it, too, is pledged against the monetary reserve, so it doesn't belong to the US. The US has only "a strategic gold reserve", and, compared to the Federal Reserve Note issue, it's miniscule.

When was "paper money" invented?

Marco Polo, in his travels to China, discovered that paper notes as large as sheets of typing paper were being used quite successfully during the reign of Kublai Khan. Grand public works projects were entirely financed with the Khan's paper currency. The traveller Polo reported that the currency "circulated in every part of the grand khan's dominions, nor dares any person, at peril of his life, refuse to accept it in payment." Shortly after 1300, as the Khan's empire itself was weakening, the Khan's paper notes fell into disuse.

When did paper money begin in Europe?

Although intrigued by the Khan's system, Europeans did not get involved with paper currency until well into the 17th Century. As a by-product of the Reformation there commenced the widespread accumulation of wealth, and starting after 1660, some people began to look for places of safekeeping. The practice started of taking one's gold to a goldsmith and paying him a small fee to keep it secure. The goldsmith, in turn, would issue the owner of the gold a receipt, a small slip of paper promising to return his gold upon demand. The process was the same as baggage checking today. When the holders of these receipts realized that others in the community would readily accept them as payment for goods and services, paper money was born.

How did "the banking system" begin?

Eventually, the goldsmith discovered that few people were actually bringing their cash receipts back to him to exchange them for the precious metals which they represented. Knowing that his bluff would not be called, the goldsmith would print up extra receipts for gold that he in fact had not received, then loan those receipts out into the community at interest. By learning how to create and loan bogus receipts in excess of the gold he actually kept on hand, and not "get caught", the goldsmiths of old became the world's first bankers. Their fraudulent actions served as the model for the "fractional reserve" banking system. By the late 18th century it was common practice for bankers to print four times as many paper receipts as they had gold deposits.

When did paper currency first appear in America?

The first paper money experiment occurred in the New World in the Massachusetts Bay Colony. William of Orange, former Captain General of the Dutch forces, waged war in Canada from 1689 to 1697. It was called King William's War. He financed it with paper money issued against the Massachusetts Bay colony. He levied heavy taxes on Colonists, and allowed a five-percent premium for all taxes paid with these notes. In other words, if a Colonist's tax due was ten shillings, he could pay it off with nine and one-half shillings' worth of William's notes.

What were "gold certificates" and "silver certificates?"

These were circulating documents which represented, and could be exchanged for, actual amounts of gold or silver guaranteed to be on deposit in the Treasury of the United States. Gold Certificates were confiscated by Presidential order in 1933, and Silver Certificates lost their redeemability in 1968, although they still were accepted at face value for all public and private debts. Even in the face of these blatant repudiations, the U.S. Government officially maintains that it has never defaulted on its monetary obligations.

Who was behind the elimination of gold and silver certificates?

The Federal Reserve banks successfully eliminated gold and silver certificates. Our money, which was always backed by a specific amount of gold and silver, is now backed by nothing. It is literally worth only the paper it's printed on.

Will the New Currency completely replace the previous issues?

In a Bill introduced into Congress on January 1, 1995 called "The Counterfeiting and Money Laundering Deterrence Act of 1995", it has been written that "international organizations hostile to the United States have produced counterfeits of the United States $100 bill that are extremely difficult to detect". The Bill also includes the following line: "Forcing international narcotics traffickers to exchange all of their hard currency held in United States $100 bills within a specified period of time for a new, counterfeit-resistant currency would significantly raise the cost of money laundering to drug cartels, thereby reducing their profits." Furthermore, the proposed Congressional Bill orders that: "The United States Treasury shall not recognize $100 denomination United States currency issued prior to the date that is 12 months after the date of enactment of this section... and such currency shall not constitute legal tender for any debt, public or private." While this Bill has not yet been enacted, the intention of the legislation seems clear: To protect the US from massive ongoing foreign counterfeit operations, and to snuff out the underground economy. Therefore, the old money must be recalled. If you have cash under a mattress or in a safety deposit box, you're going to have to exchange it for the new cash, and you may have to prove exactly where it came from to avoid confiscation by authorities.

Is the new currency detectable by remote scanning equipment?

The Bureau of Engraving and Printing has acknowledged that the new currency is magnetically encoded. The advent of MRI (Magnetic Resonance Imaging) makes for the remote detection of distinct magnetic signatures. Such machines, while expensive, are commonplace in hospitals throughout the country. Remote warrantless searches have not been found by the courts to be violations of the 4th Amendment. I suspect that searches for "illegal cash" will likewise be sanctioned by the courts. Several privacy experts maintain that the police and other authorities, (including banks, which now have been deputized into government spying), have the technology to locate and count our paper currency in our wallets and purses with remote detectors. If the sensors are designed just to find magnetic ink, any age note could be found. The new currency actually contains less magnetic ink than the pre-1990 Federal Reserve notes. If the sensors are ultra-sensitive to determine the code on each bill, I can't imagine that they could not also detect the older bills as well.

How many Federal Reserve notes are in circulation, and where are they circulating?

Out of the 700 billion dollars the Fed says is printed, they can only account for 97 billion in normal channels. This means that there are 600 billion dollars "elsewhere", the majority of it outside the United States. It's estimated there's 220 billion dollars' worth of US currency now circulating in Russia. Not surprisingly, the Fed admits that it showed the new 1996 currency design to the Russian Central Bank even before they showed it to American Bankers. The Fed will do everything possible to keep those US notes in circulation overseas, as each bill they put into circulation in a foreign country costs them only three cents to have printed, but buys them one dollar's worth of foreign assets and currency. Additionally, the hundreds of billions of dollars they take in by providing US currency to foreign economies is used by the Fed for whatever purposes the Fed determines is proper, without Congressional oversight. By law they need not provide accountings of their foreign monetary operations. Their only legal obligation is to remit to the US Treasury whatever portion of those hundreds of billions of dollars remains after they are done using the funds.

Why does more US currency circulate outside the US than inside the US?

US currency serves as local currency in many foreign countries. According to Federal Reserve Board Governor Lindsay, more 100 dollar bills circulate in the former Soviet Union than anywhere else on earth.

Isn't that a threat to our economy?

Historically, governments at war with each other have attempted to undermine each other's currency. Revolutionary War or Continental Dollars were heavily counterfeited by the British. England's pound notes were routinely counterfeited by Germany during World War two, and recent Middle Eastern wars have witnessed similar events. Having a large supply of an enemy's currency creates the ability to engage in economic warfare that can be more devastating than physical warfare. It is difficult to imagine the effect that 220 billion dollars, rapidly spent into circulation, would produce. Something on the order of post-World War One inflation would result.

Are United States Notes issued today?

United States Notes issued at one time in denominations from one to ten-thousand dollars are no longer current under law, per section 602-G14 of the Riegle Community Redevelopment and Regulatory Improvement Act of 1994. This misleadingly named

Act was used to demonetize the last remaining United States Notes. The provision amends Title 31 of the United States Code to read: "The Secretary shall not be required to re-issue United States Currency Notes upon redemption." The provision officially authorizes what has already taken place. United States Notes are no longer issued. Additionally, the 1994 Act repeals "obsolete provisions of statutory law that govern the deposit and return of US bonds that back a national bank's circulating notes." Federal Reserve notes are currently the only authorized form of paper currency issued by the Treasury, through the Federal Reserve. According to the legislation, Section 602 "makes numerous technical changes to the Federal Banking Statutes, including eliminating obsolete statutes that govern the issuance, replacement, redemption and failure to redeem circulating notes issued by National Banks." The proposal was part of a joint Congressional Conference report which became Public Law 103-325 on September 20th, with President Clinton's signature. There is no question that the folks in Congress knew exactly what they were doing, and whom they were doing it for, when they officially cancelled the last remaining United States Notes.

Would the Federal Reserve Bank object if Congress decided that United States Notes should replace their notes?

The Fed has stated that they are not as concerned with the paper money supply as they are with the electronic money supply, because the paper money supply is only 500 billion dollars, while the electronic supply is almost five trillion dollars. So as long as we leave them with the power to electronically create money, it shouldn't be that important. However, as the majority of our printed currency circulates outside the United States, (thereby providing an interest-free loan to the Federal Reserve), they would probably raise objections to the issuance of US notes.

What are "Susie Certificates"?

The Treasury is currently storing 785 million Susan B. Anthony Dollar coins (which Americans refuse to use). As these coins do not belong to the Federal Reserve Bank, it would be possible for the Treasury to print paper notes backed by these dollar coins (at a cost of three cents per note), then use these "Susie Certificates" to redeem 785 million dollars' worth of outstanding Government bonds. Such certificates would read; "Payable on Demand - One Susan B. Anthony Dollar".

Who was William of Orange?

William of Orange issued the charter to William Patterson which established the First Bank of England in 1694. William of Orange, upon ascending to the throne, immediately handed over Britain's sovereign right of currency issuance to banker and business entrepreneur Patterson. Some maintain that William of Orange gave away control of Britain's Treasury in exchange for being allowed to assume the throne.

What did money have to do with the Revolutionary War?

The Colonies were profit-making enterprises, chartered by the King. But the King didn't watch over everything that went on. In a trip to England, Ben Franklin mentioned that the Colonies had begun issuing their own currency and were no longer tied to the Bank of England. Naturally, the King didn't like that. There was an article from a British newspaper at the time, which stated if the new monetary system talked about in the Colonies was allowed to exist, Britain "will lose all its best minds". The fear was a strong American economy would eventually seduce Britain's most able producers. That's really what started the Revolution.

Why did the Colonies begin issuing their own currency?

Because the Colonies were required to pay for English goods and taxes with gold and silver, they didn't have enough coin or precious metal left to operate their own economy. They solved this problem by printing their own colonial scrip for trading within the colonies. The ability to create unbacked currency greatly extended the sovereign powers of the colonies. But, like any society issuing paper currency without metal backing, the Colonies were not without their inflationary cycles.

How did the Colonies put their scrip into circulation?

The Colony's legislative body passed resolutions authorizing the printing of various amounts of money to pay its bills. The Colonial Government's employees and suppliers accepted the money, and then they, in turn, would spend the colonial scrip into the local economy. That's how money was placed into circulation at that time. It was similar to the Chinese monetary system, whereby the Emperor wrote checks from his "royal checkbook", and then passed them to his suppliers and soldiers, who would in turn spend the Emperor's paper in the towns. Of course, the Emperor's checks were uncashable, and circulated as money throughout his Empire, until they were eventually remitted back to him in the form of tribute. As far as the issuance of currency today, we have a big difference from the Colonial and Chinese systems. Now there is a middleman. Imagine if the Emperor gave his checkbook to a friend, then borrowed money from him at interest. It's a silly scenario, but that's what happened. In 1913, the US Government gave its sovereign power to a banking cartel dominated by J.P. Morgan. This cartel has held the American checkbook ever since.

What British laws did the colonists violate by issuing their own notes for trade amongst the colonies?

The law stated that any time a note was issued that wasn't to be initially redeemed, interest had to be charged, as it was feared that non-interest bearing notes would be used as money and, thereby, undermine the monopoly that the Bank of England enjoyed.

Were Bills of Credit widespread in the Colonies?

Prior to the Constitution, every Colony understood the function of bills of credit and every colony used them. They issued bills of credit for everything they needed to do. If they needed a church, the church would actually issue "church money". These bills were issued for every particular function, including the financing of their armed forces or municipal works projects.

How were Colonial bills of credit worded?

On March 5, 1776, the city of New York decided to build a water system. They issued two thousand notes in order to do it. The notes issued stated, "The current mayor of the Colony of New York, this note shall entitle the bearer to the sum of eight shillings current money of the Colony of New York payable on demand by the Mayor, Alderman, and Commonalty of the City of New York, Office of the Chancellor, dated this fifth day of March, 1776". There was no discount on these notes, and no interest. They needed the waterworks built, they needed the two-thousand dollars, so on that particular week, month, and year they issued that note. They were paid out to the contractors and laborers, and the contractors accept them based on the fact these notes would be accepted as payment for taxes. And the contractor would have no trouble paying the grocer with this note, because the grocer owed taxes, too. The contractor would get a hundred of these notes and he would pay his workers with it and they would walk around town spreading them out and everyone living in that particular jurisdiction would accept them. Another example is the wording contained on an "indented bill" issued in 1709 which states, "receivable for taxes without interest, this indented bill of Five Shillings due from the Colony of New York, due to the possessor thereof, shall be in value equal to money and shall be accordingly acceptable by the Treasurer of this Colony for time being in all Public Payments, or for any fund at any time in the Treasury. Dated New York, 31st May, 1709."

Were there time limitations on the conversion of these notes?

Some had redemption dates, and some did not. That was the King's problem with them, because the Colonists would just continue to circulate them, and cities would continue to pay them out. Theoretically, once the cities received the notes back as payment of taxes, they were supposed to destroy them. Many times this did not happen. New York had a habit of issuing general bills of credit. They were probably the leader in the idea. They would issue general bills of credit for military, municipal, or for state expenses without addressing what they were for. Thus, there was no bank that was attached to them.

Were banks at that time able to do the same thing?

Yes, and as a matter of fact that was Alexander Hamilton's main theme. He wanted to establish a central bank and give it a monopoly on issuing such notes. But these notes weren't issued just by banks. They could be issued by individuals as well - individuals of "good standing". The most famous person in a particular county could issue his notes, and depending upon his standing and reputation, these notes would circulate within his county. Good solid "names" could issue however many notes the market would accept. "Societies" could do this as well. I came across a note from "The Society of Mechanics at Hudson".

How would a society of mechanics be able to issue notes and spend them into circulation?

It was possible because of the ability of mechanics to accept those notes as payment for their own services. These notes were as good as money in an industrial era when anything was possible. Many banks issued their own notes, from the bank of Albany to the Washington Bank in Rhode Island. Everybody, from companies to private citizens, had the ability to issue notes, as long as they could get others to accept them. There are laws prohibiting such activity today. They call it counterfeiting. You can't issue anything that is denominated in dollars. You could call them "pretend dollars". The Legal Tender Laws changed the ability of private parties to issue notes. If we could eliminate those laws, the country would be in better shape. We could let the American people use what they wanted as money. With the passage of the Legal Tender Laws, Americans were forced to accept Federal Reserve notes. The element of free choice was removed. But ideally, in theory, if you had a million ounces of gold in the ground, there should be nothing wrong with issuing your own notes if you could get people to accept them, and you were able to pay that gold out. But obviously, this isn't the case. That would be honest money, and it would cut the Federal Reserve out. That's what the Legal Tender Laws were all about, handing the Fed a money monopoly.

Early in the Nation's history, did the existence of so many different types of notes produce inflation?

In many instances, yes. Let's say you build a bridge, and you issue tax credit certificates called "bridge certificates". When the bridge is done, these bills are still circulating, and they get turned into the Treasury every so often. The Treasurer, at his discretion, could re-issue these notes, because as the Treasurer, he knows what the area's financial needs are. So, in the early days of the Colonies, they didn't necessarily bring the currency in and retire it. If the tax collector in the City of New York received a water note in payment of his issue, he could just as well choose to circulate the note again. He might just as easily put it back into usage as tear it up, especially if he wasn't the issuing authority. When you calculate how many projects were undertaken with specific note issues, over a period of years, you can see the great potential for inflation.

How did the Colonial Treasurer know whether to send a note back into circulation or tear it up?

By studying his record of issue, and by knowing how many were still outstanding, and when they were going to expire. Some of them had expiration dates after which they were no good. His decision is based on the specific circumstances at the time he comes into possession of the notes. Let's assume that the Treasurer anticipated receiving only one-tenth of a note issue back in the first year, and instead, the entire issue shows up in the first year. Then he has a problem. He has to use those notes as money because he was anticipating that payments 90 per cent of his revenues for the year would be paid with actual money. In that case he has to recirculate the notes, as the Treasury has nothing else to pay its own bills with.

How did the Treasurer keep track of where all the outstanding notes were?

When the note was issued, the Treasurer had to keep a chart with numbers. Every one of the notes was numbered, so he knew how many were issued and how many were still outstanding. He kept a journal and every individual note had an individual number. He could tell by looking at his journal how many had been redeemed and how many were outstanding. Using his discretion to help regulate or stimulate the economy, he had the authority to destroy, extend, or even issue a different type of note.

Did the Treasurer have sole authority to issue notes from the Treasury?

The Treasurer didn't have the authority to issue the notes unless he was authorized to do so. He couldn't, at his discretion, issue notes. There had to be an act of the appropriate parliament authorizing the issue, specifying how much was to be issued, and the dates it would circulate. Only after he had received this could the Treasurer issue notes. When he received authorization, then the mechanics of it were left to him. How and where he did it, which ones he circulated, and which ones were kept back - these things were left to his judgement, based on his financial needs as the Treasurer. He might be balancing a water issue along with a bridge issue and a tunnel issue and a general revenue issue. If he were anticipating a certain quantity of one note and didn't get it, he could substitute it with a quantity of the second note. He doesn't necessarily have to destroy the notes before the date the legislature has ordered him to do so.

Who was charged with the fiscal well-being of the town or municipality?

The local legislatures. That's the idea of local law. And the wisdom of their fiscal management either got them into office or got them thrown out.

Were the Colonists astute enough to elect legislators who could properly administer their economic needs?

Yes, clearly they were. That's why removing the phrase "and emit bills of credit" from the Constitution resulted in such a heated debate. The Colonists realized that their own ability to create circulating notes, via their elected representatives, was of vital importance. Of course, they also knew such bills could be tremendously inflated, but in such cases, they were free to accept them or not.

Did the ability of the citizens to "reject" certain note issues become a problem for the Legislatures?

Yes, and this matter was first addressed with the Queen Anne Proclamation of 1704. Statutes were invoked if someone refused payment in these notes. As a matter of fact, in Virginia, the punishment was very severe. I know that in South Carolina, if one didn't accept them, it resulted in a seizure. These would be known today as legal tender laws. After Queen Anne's Proclamation of 1704, virtually every single Colony did the same thing.

If you had a note from one colony, how was it treated in a neighboring colony?

That was the point of Queen Anne's Proclamation. Massachusetts Bay was the first colony to issue paper money, and she tried by proclamation to force the Colony of New York to accept the Massachusetts Bay emissions. Once they had declared their independence, however, there was nothing in the Articles of Confederation to force one State to accept another State's money.

What currency would the Colonials use to do business with a person in another colony?

Certainly not with paper money of your colony. The paper notes weren't meant to completely replace specie payment or real money. A bill of credit was clearly distinguished from money. We were in a time when a Colony was never really granted any rights to issue coin currency. There was no legal coinage of that time. Bills of credit were paper issues that were really a temporary "borrowing", although they took on the form and function of money.

What's the difference between a "bill of credit" and a "bill of exchange"?

A bill of exchange represents a tangible item, and a bill of credit represents an intangible item. A bill of credit is potential and a bill of exchange is actual. A bill of exchange certifies that a transaction has taken place. It was mostly used for import and export, or if one was sending something across a great distance and it would take some time to get there. A bill of exchange was an international payment, sort of a bearer-bond of the time. It was primarily because of tobacco and the other exports that bills of exchange were first established. They differed slightly from bills of credit, which represented something that hadn't occurred yet, as bills of exchange represented something that had actually taken place. Bills of credit represented anticipated events, as in the case of taxes, or in the case of a merchant with goods that he hadn't sold yet. Bills of exchange were used extensively in Virginia, and were backed by actual stores of tobacco sitting in warehouses.

What was "Tobacco Money"?

In Virginia, tobacco was money. In fact, that's how the farmers were taxed. The "tax collector" would go out to the farms and make the farmers burn some of their tobacco, the purpose being to reduce the supply of available tobacco. It helped support the price of the existing tobacco stored in the warehouse. The legislature was the body responsible for making the determination of how much to burn, and it was quite an unpopular event. Virginia is the model that I use, because their entire economy was tobacco, and they were the first Colony to establish a public tobacco warehouse that issued these bills of exchange for tobacco deposits. The Colonial farmer would show up at the warehouse with his tobacco, and there was an official tobacco inspector who would look at the tobacco, then store it in the public's warehouse, and give the farmer a "tobacco certificate". This certificate was, in fact, a bill of exchange. One exchanged his tobacco for these certificates. It was more like a receipt that was completely negotiable. Because the warehouse was publicly administered by a publicly-elected person, there was confidence in that system. These tobacco certificates, at least in Virginia, were as good as money. As a matter of fact, Virginia was the last Colony to turn to the issue of unbacked paper money, because these bills of exchange filled the void. Virginia had no need for unbacked currency, since there was plenty of their tobacco money to go around.

What was the Triangle Slave Trade?

A triangular route of rum, sugar and slave trade between the West Indies, Europe, and the Colonies. The Triangle trade provided for a solid base of wealth in the Providence Plantations of Rhode Island and in Charleston, South Carolina, but the real wealth from this trading flowed into entry ports in Philadelphia and New York - Manhattan, in particular. Had New Orleans or Charleston or some other city been the recipient of profits from the Triangle trade, the world would be a different place today. We'd have a different financial center. It was the concentration of wealth and financial power residing in New York City at the time that was behind the elimination of the Federal Government's ability to emit bills of credit. This power center also had clear interests in seeing that mortgages were not cancelled, all debts were honored, and that the slave trade was not interrupted. If you read Jefferson's writings, (contrary to what they say about him), you can see that he abhorred slavery. So did George Washington. The people who were really in there fighting, for the most part, were not pro-slavery. America was not a nation of slave holders. Absent the machinations of the New York money center, slavery would have died all by itself, but that's a separate issue.

Who is supposed to issue our currency, per the Constitution?

According to Article One, Section Eight of the Constitution, "The Congress shall have the power to coin money, regulate the value thereof, and of foreign coin, and affix the standard of weights and measures".

How does our current system of money creation differ from the system envisioned by the framers of the Constitution?

Under the system of our Forefathers, our currency was very strictly defined. With Constitutional money, when you were paid for goods and services, your payment was immediate and tangible. It required the movement of a fixed supply commodity, namely, gold or silver of a particular weight and fineness. And if the standard value of the dollar were changed, it would have to be done by Congress and on record. Additionally, all Government or private borrowing resulted in the lender being repaid with dollars that were worth the same as those that he lent. Thomas Jefferson recognized that if the Government was too abusive in its spending patterns, the people could vote with their money by withdrawing it from circulation. This reality imposed a degree of fiscal prudence upon the Politicians by limiting the supply of dollars from which to borrow. Under the current system, no such constraints exist. When our Government spends more than it takes in, it is not limited to the amount of money people choose to lend it, as it has created its own private bank which extends to it unlimited credit.

Why did the framers of the Constitution deny Congress the ability to "emit bills of credit"?

Mindful of the inflationary woes that paper money created in Europe and the Colonies, it was ultimately agreed that the new government should be denied the power to issue paper currency in the form of "bills of credit", which were circulating promissory notes redeemable in gold and silver. However, many argued strongly in favor of giving Congress the right to issue such bills, knowing that in times of war and other emergencies it was sometimes necessary to increase the Treasury's money supply to make needful purchases. They also knew that during such monetary emergencies, lacking the ability to temporarily issue and circulate such bills, the Government would be forced to borrow from private banks, thereby becoming exposed to the very same paper-related treacheries as they were attempting to avoid. Observing that the phrase "emit bills of credit" was excluded from Congress's enumerated powers in the Constitution's final draft, James Madison lamented, "We snatched defeat from the jaws of victory". Madison knew that by denying the new Government the ability to occasionally create interest-free paper which could be circulated as currency, the sovereignty of the young Republic would eventually become jeopardized through inevitable borrowing and indebtedness to private banking consortiums, who would eagerly loan the Government (at interest) the very paper that Government could have itself created.

Were secret societies involved in shaping the Constitution's provisions for the American monetary system?

There was Freemasonry's link, via Ben Franklin. Edmund Randolph had a hand in the provision that required the Colonies to honor the full value of the War debt to the bankers. The most crucial provision was that the new Government not be allowed to emit bills of credit, which would compete with the Banking families' ability to issue and lend fiat money. The prohibition against paper currency forced America to use only gold and silver coin in all its transactions. Everyone present at the Constitutional Convention was familiar with Marco Polo's accounting of how paper money was successfully used in China. They understood that a sovereign body could issue its own currency, and use it quite successfully. But the banking interests didn't want the Government to be in competition with them. So after considerable debate, the Constitution was drafted, prohibiting anything but gold and silver coin to be lawful currency. The Federalist Papers, along with Madison's account of the Constitutional debates, really give historians a good feel as to who was representing the Foreign Banking interests during this formative period in developing America's monetary policies.

Why was Congress originally given the power to fix and regulate the value of currency?

The Founding Fathers knew that it was imperative that monetary values remained constant. They understood that without monetary stability it would be impossible to save for the future.

Why did the framers of the Constitution choose gold and silver coins as the "currency of the realm"?

The reason that gold and silver were chosen as denominators was because of the limited supply of these metals, as well as their unique characteristics of division and durability. Having experienced the inflation that paper money produced, they wanted to ensure that the new Government was limited in its ability to create money, and precious metal inherently provided the necessary constraints.

Was precious metal money favored by the general population?

Yes. In fact, the Dollar's value actually rose in rough times. Additionally, because the Government was required to reduce the metal content in a coin each time they reduced the underlying unit's (dollar's) value, people could actually watch their dollars strengthen or weaken. This fact allowed citizens to vote with their money.

What is meant by "voting with money"?

If a Government issues its currency, then relinquishes control of it and allows the free market to determine its value (as in the case of gold coins), then people can "vote with their money" in choosing to finance public projects by either "loaning" their gold and silver coins to the Government, or by keeping their coins. The former, of course, is a vote of confidence in that project or administration, and it stimulates growth. The latter is a no-confidence vote, and would generally cause a slowdown in growth, perhaps even a depression, thereby generating a clean sweep at the polls. Only worthy or profitable projects would be considered under this system, as each Government project would have to seek financing in private markets like all others.

How did the Founding Fathers feel about the Banking Industry?

Thomas Jefferson perhaps best summed up the prevalent feeling when he said, "If the American people ever allow private banks to control the issue of their currency, first by inflation and then by deflation, the banks and the corporations that will grow up around them will deprive the people of all property until their children wake up homeless on the continent their Fathers conquered. "

Do Americans surrender any Constitutional rights by accepting and using Federal Reserve Notes?

When we utilize the notes of a private corporation as a vehicle to discharge our debts, we unknowingly adhere ourselves to a complete body of contractual law that exists and operates outside the Constitution. Under Common Law, the maxim is that you enter a contract knowingly, with full knowledge, and unless you have full knowledge of every provision of the contract, you can't even enter it. However, under Admiralty Law (or Maritime Law, or Military Law), you can enter into a contract which is known as an implied contract without your consent. And unless you question the jurisdiction or the assumption that you've entered into that contract, then you have consented. It's that simple. Our acceptance and use of Federal Reserve notes removes us from Constitutional protections, and into a host of implied contractual obligations, most of which are unknown to the general population.

How did US citizens move into an "Admiralty jurisdiction" by their acceptance of unbacked currencies?

In 1861, Abraham Lincoln created his "Greenbacks", thereby allowing a citizen to discharge debts not with what the Constitution called legal tender, but with what Lincoln called legal tender. Title 50 United States Code, section 213 created a Maritime Jurisdiction in the District of Columbia. This allowed for the issuance of "Greenbacks", which were not lawful money according to the Constitution. Consequently, Americans were given the ability to "discharge their debts" with these "Greenbacks" instead of demanding payment in lawful money. The second move into Admiralty jurisdiction was brought about by the establishment of the Federal Reserve Banking system. Essentially, "we the people" established this Federal Reserve Bank, and as "stockholders" or as "shareholders" we vote our shares through our voting in the general elections. The people are the stockholders of the Government, in fact, and if you "vote your share" by electing your CEO, then you've entered into another adhesion contract that you didn't know about. By our action of voting for President, we become part of this "corporate United States". We are not State Citizens anymore, but have declared ourselves to be "Federal" Citizens simply by voting for a President.

Is the United States officially bankrupt?

Yes, without question. It's contained in Senate Report 93-549. It's on the record. The US was declared bankrupt in 1934 and again in 1950. We've never recovered.

Did any administrative changes occur as a result of the US bankruptcy?

All of the Article 3 courts have become Article 1 legislative tribunals. There ceased to be common law courts - instead we have commerical law ruling the Judicial system.

How was this administrative changeover put into effect?

That's where you get into the Trading with the Enemy Act. That is the peg on which they hung their hat, this 1917 Act which was amended in 1933. They brought the 1917 Act up to date by redefining whom it applied to - namely, us. Prior to 1933, it did not apply to citizens of the United States.

Is there any legislation on record which states, "All Common Law courts are hereby cancelled due to a continuing emergency?"

No, the orchestrators wouldn't be that blatant. They simply converted Common Law courts into Admiralty courts. The first thing they did was create the Admiralty jurisdiction. The second thing they did was extend the Admiralty jurisdiction. The third thing was to overlap the two jurisdictions. Then, finally, they removed the Common Law jurisdiction altogether. The 1937 Erie versus Tompkins decision recognized America's conversion to a new type of jurisdiction when the Supreme Court stated, "There is no Federal Common Law". Basically, that one statement eroded all Common Law protections.

Was there ever any discussion by the Constitution's framers prohibiting the Government from accumulating bonded debt?

No. At that time, the removal of the ability to issue bills was the issue. Bonds were never a question. Thomas Jefferson wanted to forbid all forms of debt because he thought debt was a fatal disease, but no one put forth any specific provision to outlaw bonds. In the Articles of Confederation, the ability to emit bills of credit was a power given to Congress. That provision placed the money power back into the hands of the Government, which is where it belonged. But by failing to include this ability in the Constitution's list of enumerated Congressional powers, it resulted in the same nonsense that has occurred throughout history, whereby governments would be forced to turn to private bankers for their monetary supply.

Did omitting the phrase "to emit bills of credit" from the Constitution prohibit the States from issuing bills of credit under their own authority?

Under the Tenth Amendment, theoretically, you could argue that it was reserved. I've tried to get into that argument without much success. My contention is that all powers not given to the Federal government are reserved to the people and the States, and that would mean that a State should have the ability to emit bills of credit. People point simply to the clause, "No State shall make anything but gold or silver legal tender for payment of debt". If it wasn't carefully laid out, it was the most provident mistake ever made.

Who at the Constitutional Convention can be pointed to as being responsible for denying Congress the ability to issue bills of credit?

I believe a group of Masons was sent to subvert the Articles of Confederation into this anomaly called the "Constitution of the United States". They had two primary interests. Their first objective was to protect the slave holders and slave traders based in Rhode Island and South Carolina. Their second objective was to ensure that all debts incurred during the Revolution, and the mortgages held by British subjects on American properties, were honored and repaid. They skillfully accomplished both objectives, which was quite a task, as the majority of the Colonial leaders, the ones who actually physically fought the war, fully intended to cancel all debts owed to British interests. One can get a sense of the intrigue going on at the time by reading not only the notes taken during the Constitutional debates, but by studying the Anti-Federalist papers and the Federalist papers. It's important to know the background of those who attended and whom each was in fact representing. Edmund Randolph, being the prime agent of this destruction, understood more than anyone there what he was doing. And Hamilton's arguments make perfect sense when you understand that his objective was to establish a central bank, and in order to make his deal, he was willing to give in on other issues to those representing the slave trade.

How was the first "central bank" established?

King William of Orange borrowed 12 million pounds in bank notes from a well-connected entrepreneur named William Patterson. Patterson's bank had no assets to back up the loan. Therefore, to ensure the notes would be accepted by his soldiers and the English people, the King granted Patterson a charter establishing the First Bank of England, thereby backing Patterson's notes with the full faith and credit of the English government.

Was the Bank of England connected to the establishment of the First Bank of the United States?

Alexander Hamilton, the major advocate for creating a central bank for the newly-formed united States, was a partner with Bank of England founder William Patterson in several business ventures. While it is uncertain whether Hamilton received financial support from Patterson or the Bank of England in exchange for his lobbying efforts for an American Central bank, it is a matter of public record that Patterson and his heirs were part of the clique that established the First and Second Banks of the United States, as well as the Bank of New York.

How long after the drafting of the Constitution was the First Bank of the United States established?

Four years. It didn't take long at all. The First Bank of the

United States was chartered even before the US Mint was established. Before the first coins rolled out of the mint, the bankers were already printing fiat money. That's what prompted Madison to say, "We have clinched defeat from the jaws of victory". The bankers' hold lasted until Andrew Jackson successfully ended their reign, in 1836.

What was the earliest American Central Bank?

Central banking actually began with the Bank of North America in 1781. This bank had always been able to issue notes and keep them recorded as "this note is equal to one dollar in silver". It had always been able to pay its obligations without a problem, so they were given a charter to exist. The National government was actually a stockholder in it. Congress incorporated the First Bank of the United States. It was ours; we actually owned part of that one. The bank had an office of discount, an office of deposit, and the bank of the United States was available to just about anyone. The Constitution didn't specify anything about incorporating banks, so those powers would be reserved to the States and to the people. There were a lot of State banks, but on a National level, the First Bank of the United States was it.

Was there any debate in the courts regarding the Constitutionality of the United States establishing a bank?

No, absolutely not. It was a private bank. That was in 1781. By 1791 the Bank of North America had taken on the image of the United States to such an extent that when they chartered the First Bank of the United States in 1791, no one challenged that, either. The Government was a share-holder, a stock holder. At that time, the United States was not "the United States, a corporate entity". That provision of the Constitution had not yet been fully exploited.

Could the Government Constitutionally enter itself into the banking business?

There was nothing in the Constitution prohibiting the Federal Government from entering into commercial arrangements. As a matter of fact, years later, the Clearfield Doctrine was issued, specifying that when the Government introduces itself as a commercial entity, it must comply with the rules that any other commercial entity follows. It can't cite sovereign immunity, or any other privileges. It has to act as if it were a commercial entity.

Should State banks be allowed to issue their own notes?

No. I agree that the Federal Government should regulate note issue. I think that the Federal Government should have the ability to tell the state how much they can issue, and I have no problem with a central issuing authority. If a State decides that it needs to issue a million dollars in order to build a bridge, it should work with the Federal government, who should do the actual issuing.

Why was J.P. Morgan regarded as the most powerful man in the early 20th Century?

In December of 1909, J.P. Morgan purchased a majority stake in Equitable Life Insurance, which gave him strong influence over three insurance companies, including New York Life. His Banker's Trust had taken over three other banks. In 1909 he gained control of Guarantee Trust, which, through a series of mergers, converted into America's largest trust. The core money trust group then included J.P. Morgan, First National Bank, and National City Bank. Some banks had so many overlapping directors they were hard to separate. Banks held large equity stakes in each other. Why didn't banks just merge instead of carrying on a charade? Most were private partnerships or closely owned banks. The answer harkens back to the traditional American antipathy against concentrated financial power. The Morgan-First National-National City trio would run into powerful public opposition if they openly declared an alliance.

What were the "Pujo hearings"?

In 1907 we had the Pujo hearings. There was an attempt to reveal the existence of a money trust. Thomas Lamont was asked, "Is it true that fifty people control the wealth of the United States?" He said that was absolute nonsense. He knew for a fact that there were only twelve people who controlled American wealth. Today, we are quite used to the notion that an elite group of bankers controls the economy. It's been written about many times and everyone knows about it. In that early period, it came as quite a shock to most. The most vocal critics of the Banking Trust were not called during the Pujo Hearings. Instead, the Committee called J.P. Morgan. They made a circus out of it. They finally came to a conclusion that there was indeed a money trust. There is a great book called "The Money Changers" which details how the Money Trust caused the money panic of 1907. These Pujo hearings came to the conclusion that the Money Trust was creating and influencing finance with their bank notes, and with their abilities to influence each others' actions.

What was the outcome of the Pujo hearings?

It was decided that power should be taken away from J.P. Morgan and given to a new government-regulated banking authority.

Were the Pujo hearings "staged" by the bankers?

Arsene Pujo, the man sponsoring the hearing, was closely allied with the oil trust and the Rockefellers. The banking families wanted to give the public an appearance of reform. Their real intention was to stop the influence of rival banks, especially the Southern banks. The Southern banking industry was really starting to compete in a big way. Southern farmers no longer had to run to New York to get their money. But it wasn't just the Southern banks that the New York crowd was after. They wanted to take the power to create money away from all other private banks.

Did any member of Congress realize that the Pujo hearings were "staged"?

Congressman Charles Lindbergh, Sr. knew full well how the banker's game worked. He remarked, "Ever since the Civil War, Congress has allowed the bankers to control financial legislation. Membership of the Finance Committee in the Senate and the Committee on Banking and Currency in the House has been made up of bankers, their agents and their attorneys. These Committees have controlled the nature of bills to be recorded, the extent of them, and the debates that should be held on them when they are being considered in the Senate and the House. No one not on the Committee has recognized that".

How did the establishment of the Federal Reserve Bank eliminate competition from the rapidly-growing Southern banks?

By removing their ability to independently issue notes. The real ability of Southern banks to threaten the New York Banks was their ability to issue notes that the local people would accept in exchange for commercial contracts that farmers had in cotton. Lets say I'm a farmer and I'm planting cotton, and I have an order for cotton from Europe. I then go to the Southern Cotton Bank, and they issue notes against my contract for the cotton based on my standing in the cotton industry. Basically it was the same thing that the Colonies were doing in the 1690's. The establishment of a Central Reserve Bank staffed with principals, employees and allies of the New York banking trust guaranteed the elimination of competition from all banks outside the New York clique.

What was the economic climate immediately prior to the passage of the Federal Reserve Act?

In the early 1900's, Americans experienced one banking panic after another. After the "Panic of 1907", everyone had enough. Of course, no one realized that the wave of panics and bank failures, especially the 1907 panic, were carefully planned by the bankers themselves. The tactic of creating a panic, then going out and buying business and real estate for pennies was "the Rothschild tradition". So after 1907, the public clamored for regulation and stability, and the bankers turned around and gave them the Federal Reserve System.

Did citizens object to various changes in the gold and silver content of the coins they used?

Congress officially reduced the gold content of a five-dollar gold piece, but that did nothing to the value of the five dollar gold piece someone owned previous to the change. As a matter of fact, it enhanced its value. Whenever such a reduction of gold content was made in US coins, the older gold coins would be melted and the gold removed, as the face value was exceeded by the coin's metal content. This added to the scarcity of the older coins.

Did FDR's Executive Order require all gold in America be turned in to the Banks?

The Executive Order listed specific categories of gold that were exempt from confiscation: "Such amount of gold as may be required for legitimate and customary use in industry, profession, or art within a reasonable time." Also exempt were "gold coin and gold certificates in an amount not exceeding in the aggregate of 100 dollars belonging to any one person", and "gold coins having a recognized special value to collectors of rare and unusual coin." This last exemption is why those who wish to invest in gold often choose rare US coins over "bullion coins" such as the Maple Leaf and the Krugerrand. If the US Government confiscated gold again, the collector would be allowed to keep his gold in the form of rare US coins.

Why did the Federal Reserve instruct Roosevelt to confiscate the American people's gold coins?

The dollar notes we gave to Europe, having nowhere else to go, made their way back here in the 1920s, and were redeemed for what the European bankers and investors understood was lawful money of the United States, twenty-dollar gold pieces and the like. (Numismatists know that Europe is the present-day source of twenty dollar gold pieces, and some very rare dates come out of there today. It's primarily European banks that have them). The investors and bankers in Europe cashed in all their US paper currency throughout the 1920's, to the point where, in 1928, it became apparent there were far more notes printed than there was gold available to back them up.   America's coins were disappearing, and by 1933 Roosevelt had to issue an Executive Order stating that Americans holding gold bullion must turn it in to the Federal Reserve, and after a specified date, Americans would no longer be able to own gold.

Why was US Currency devalued after Roosevelt's Executive Order?

The year after the recall, gold rose to thirty-five dollars per ounce.   This was done to adjust the value of the notes in circulation to the actual gold supply.   There were few who understood the actual reason for the devaluation, which was that the Federal Reserve had nearly doubled the supply of paper money during World War One, sending most of it overseas to protect British Banking interests.   When that money returned home, American citizens had to pay the full penalty of the Fed's imprudence through an overnight forty-percent reduction of their dollar's purchasing power, and surrender of their Constitutional currency.

Did the Federal Reserve learn its lesson and stop inflating the money supply after the 1934 devaluation of the Dollar?

On the contrary, by prohibiting citizens from owning gold, and by cancelling the US citizen's ability to redeem Federal Reserve Notes with gold, the Federal Reserve was free to create additional notes for its own purposes and projects with virtually no fear of depressionary repercussions. Citizens and officials were told, and believed, that every thirty-five dollars of Federal Reserve Notes were backed by one ounce of gold in the Treasury, even though no one was allowed to redeem their Fed notes for this amount. Americans trusted the notion that a fixed gold-backing existed for their currency throughout the forties and fifties. The Second World War helped out a little bit, and of course Bretton Woods gave the excess dollars that were being created a place to go. Now you had foreign nations gathering dollars to buy oil and you had economies around the world putting in a demand for dollars, which the Federal Reserve more than met. Of course, the people of the US had no knowledge of how many dollars the Fed was issuing. If those same dollars had been dumped into the domestic economy at the same rate they were being channelled to overseas markets, the inflation would have been incredible.

How did the Fed's dollars travel from the United States to bank accounts overseas?

The Federal Reserve, in those days, had no notion of electronic transfer, which began in the 1960's, so we're talking about suitcases full of cash. The dollars were carried in suitcases and physically moved. It was based on the mentality of "getting their money out". This fundamental trust of banks that we have today did not exist forty or fifty years ago. Solid bank-to-bank relationships had not been established in terms of the international banking system. The notion that you could arrive in the US, close a deal with a US firm, shake hands, and fly home to Sardinia with no worries about the money being placed in your account in the morning didn't exist. A businessman would strike a deal and be paid in cash or check, which he would cash, then take his money home. He would then deposit his dollars in his local bank, or keep the dollars in his vault, as cash. Businesses dealt in physical dollars. To them, only cash was money. It's only the recent generation that has accepted electronic credits in place of tangible money.

Would foreigners convert Dollars obtained from the United States into their local currencies?

A foreign businessman with a suitcase full of dollars could walk into his local bank and say, "I want to convert this into Lira". But in the post-World War Two economy, what was better than a dollar? Absolutely nothing. People were storing their wealth in dollars. That's the point. There was a demand for dollars which far exceeded their supply. You had a tremendous situation for both the Fed and the international business community, and the people who were storing their wealth in dollars instead of in their local currency became rich. The dollar would appreciate versus their local currency. This was a great benefit to the Federal Reserve, because they were circulating money that they generated at interest, with a lien against the United States, yet it wasn't circulating domestically and causing an inflation problem. It was the best of both worlds.

Are members of the Federal Reserve "public officials"?

No. They take no oath of office and they are not elected by the people. The entity that controls the issuance of our currency is made up of individuals who are representatives from the world's most powerful private banks.

Can the Federal Reserve Bank run out of money?

No. The Federal Reserve Bank has the exclusive power to create money in the United States. In effect, this bank has been allowed to borrow money from our collective future, and our children's and grandchildren's futures, and loan it to our present government. That is taxation without representation. Future generations will need to pay from 80 to 85 percent of their total wages to satisfy America's debt obligation.

How can the Fed "reduce the value" of the Dollar?

Federal Reserve Notes can be invisibly debased in value while you are holding them simply by increasing their supply. When the Government spends money that it doesn't collect in taxes, the Federal Reserve can simply create money instead of borrowing it from the existing supply.

What would happen if the supply of dollars was fixed and limited?

You could save money throughout your life, and every dollar you saved would retain its full purchasing power. Clearly this is currently not the case. Retaining wealth in Federal Reserve Notes is a recipe for wealth <u>deterioration</u>.

Can the Federal Reserve System continue indefinitely?

One thing to realize about our fractional reserve banking system is that, like a child's game of musical chairs, as long as the music is playing, there are no losers. As long as people who own credit dollars (these are notes that are not yet printed, but are simply "blips" in an account; mere computer entries) do not turn these "blips" into paper money, the game can continue forever.

Who owns the Federal Reserve Bank?

The Federal Reserve Banks are a privately owned consortium controlled by major stock-holding banks. This small group decides the fates of hundreds of millions of people by their financial policies and maneuvers. It was Baron Meyer Amschel Bauer Rothschild, (born in 1744 and died in 1812) who said, "Give me control over a nation's currency and I care not who makes its laws."

How did the banking cartels gain their power and control over the affairs of nations?

By means of the invention known as "interest", a system which permits parasites to amass huge fortunes from the efforts of producing members of the society.

Are Federal Reserve Notes issued by our Treasury?

Our Bureau of Engraving and Printing prints the money, and then sells it to the Federal Reserve Bank simply for the cost of the printing. The Federal Reserve bank then loans it back to our Government. The Federal Reserve also demands security to back up the loan, so Congress authorizes the Treasury to print US bonds which are given to the Federal Reserve Bank as collateral against this loan. This means that the United States has been mortgaged to a handful of international bankers.

Are Federal Reserve Notes really "dollars"?

Early in 1977, an attorney for the Treasury admitted that "Federal Reserve notes are not dollars". Although they are denominated in dollars, Federal Reserve notes are in fact merely notes for dollars. They are not dollars themselves. They are checks which are easily written but can never be cashed.

When did the Federal Reserve acquire America's gold?

When Franklin Roosevelt issued the following proclamation: "By Executive Order of The President, issued April 5, 1933, all persons are required to deliver on or before May 1, 1933, all gold coin, gold bullion, and gold certificates now owned by them, to a Federal Reserve Bank, branch, or agency, or to any member bank of the Federal Reserve System." The important thing to note is to whom FDR was demanding the gold be delivered to. It wasn't the Treasury of the United States. It was the Federal Reserve Banks. Upon receiving the gold from the Citizens, the Federal Reserve Bank simply printed additional Federal Reserve Notes to pay for the gold.

Is the Fed ever audited?

The Internal Revenue Service has no jurisdiction over the Federal Reserve Banks; therefore, it is never asked to produce its records or books. After many years of pressure, Congress required auditing by the General Accounting Office in 1976, but exempted all monetary activities from such audits. Audits are restricted to real estate and office supplies, et cetera... so at least taxpayers know how many paper clips they use!

Does the Fed pay taxes?

Unlike you and I, the Fed files no income tax return, nor does it pay any income taxes. In its eighty-plus years of existence, it has never lost money. Its assets have increased from zero in 1913 to over 100 billion dollars today.

Does the Federal Reserve attempt to influence Presidential elections?

The Federal Reserve and the administration they choose work hand-in-hand. The Fed cooperates with the President if they want him to get re-elected. Greenspan wanted to keep his position, and his recent interest rate drops have both lit the fires in the stock markets and caused unemployment rates to fall. We're seeing a Fed-created, roaring and booming economy here in 1996. The problem is that the person who has already amassed a pile of dollars and plans on getting through the next five years without losing purchasing power had really better wake up, especially if those dollars are stored in fixed return investments like bonds.

How does the Fed's monetization of the Debt affect the average consumer?

Our purchasing power is being eroded to postpone the date at which there is going to be some sort of collapse, and it's pitting the husbands against the wives. Every week my wife has her hand out for a few more dollars, but brings back the same amount of groceries. If I didn't know better, I'd be mad at her. The American people sense something isn't right. They feel their paychecks' purchasing power diminishing year after year, but they don't know whom to point their fingers at. It harkens back to the Jerry Ford administration, when he used to wear a button saying "whip inflation now!", as if "we the people" could do something about it. It's the Federal Reserve Banks, plain and simple.

Why is the Federal Reserve System considered by some to be more influential than our own Congress?

They get to decide the volume of money in America. And whoever controls the volume of money really controls the country.

Are members of the Federal Reserve Bank members of our Government?

No. Americans do not elect any member of the Federal Reserve Board. Federal Reserve employees are not civil servants, and do not take oaths of office. The Federal Reserve has no allegiance to the American people - only to itself.

Are members of the Federal Reserve Board public-spirited businessmen, acting on behalf of our best financial interests?

Without public knowledge, the Federal Reserve banks have moved behind the scenes to create money for themselves and their allies. Their activities are beyond public scrutiny, they need account to no one, and they refuse to open their books to Congressional inspection. In early 1996 an investigation was completed which uncovered what a New York Congressman publicly characterized as a "3.7 billion dollar slush fund".

Have the operations of the Federal Reserve Bank ever lost money for the American people?

The Fed's pattern of creating money, then loaning it to a questionable venture, with the American People as co-signers, is well established. The creation of corporations such as FNMA, SBA, FSLIC, FDIC, and then chaining the losses of these entities to the American people is a well-known fact. The biggest money losers are our direct grants to foreign entities and governments, whose activities are totally exempt from our scrutiny. The BCCI scandal just touched the tip of the iceberg with regard to fraud in those areas. Not one man in a thousand understands the depth of ongoing corruption in our present monetary system.

Is it Congress or the Federal Reserve bank that is to blame for the declining Dollar and huge National debt?

Our biggest threat to sovereignty stems from excesses in our monetary system. The Federal Reserve Banks are directly responsible for this excess, although they love to put the blame on Congress. The Fed's granting of credit allows Congress to spend money that isn't there.

When was the Federal Reserve Bank established?

The Federal Reserve Act institutionalized the Federal Reserve Bank on December 23rd, 1913. This piece of legislation established a "superbank", which would be the "lender of last resort" for the markets.

Is the Federal Reserve Bank a US Government agency?

As most people understand it, the Fed is part of the government. This is not the case. Nor is it entirely true that they are a private corporation. They are a cartel, and their choice of the word "Federal" is no accident. The Federal Reserve as established is indeed federal. In order to understand this, we go to Black's Law Dictionary. The word "federal" is defined as, "of or constituting a government in which power is distributed between a central authority and a number of constituent territorial units". The "central authority" referred to in Black's Law Dictionary is, in this case, the Federal Reserve Board. The "constituent territorial units" are the various Federal Reserve Banks. The Federal Reserve, as purely defined, is indeed federal. The Federal reserve banks are in fact their own masters, subservient to no one, and exist under their own jurisdiction.

Why did Congress establish the Federal Reserve Bank?

It was the direct result of a "public outcry" over the power of J.P. Morgan, the New York banking house, and Kuhn-Loeb & Co. Beginning in 1907, a "money trust hysteria" ensued after a wave of well publicized Morgan-orchestrated bank mergers. J.P. Morgan and his partners held 72 directorships in 112 banks, railroads, and utility companies. The public, learning of Morgan's monopoly over American business and finance, clamored for government regulations which they hoped might protect them against being swallowed by the giant Morgan empire. What the public had no way of knowing was that the "public outcry" for banking regulation was originated by the New York Banking trusts themselves, part of a clever maneuver to stem the power of the rapidly growing Southern and Western banks. A program was undertaken to deny this power, and to reconsolidate the interests of the Morgan crowd. The passage of the Federal Reserve Act was the end result of their plan to conquer, by regulation, the banking system of the United States.

How did the Federal Reserve Bank persuade citizens to use Federal Reserve Notes, instead of gold and silver coin?

At the time the Federal Reserve came into existence, the people had plenty of experience with losing their hard-earned dollars to banks which did not have the assets to back their promises. To them, the Federal Reserve Bank was "just another bank". For this reason, the officials of the Federal Reserve Bank had to ensure that their notes could be redeemed for gold. Therefore, the notes bore the following phrase; "This note is receivable by all National and member banks and Federal Reserve Banks, and for all taxes, customs, and other public dues. It is redeemable in gold on demand at the Treasury Department of the United States in the city of Washington, District of Columbia, or in gold or lawful money at any Federal Reserve Bank". When the citizens found that they could in fact exchange the new notes for gold, the notes became widely accepted.

Does our current Federal Reserve Note contain a promise to pay gold?

No. The current Federal Reserve note contains no written promise to pay anything. 1914 to 1934 was the only period during which Federal Reserve notes were redeemable in gold. It is interesting to note that the Federal Reserve Bank persuaded the United States government to agree to redeem their privately issued notes with gold. The Federal Reserve banks made the profit by issuing the notes and loaning them out for interest, but the Treasury, which made no profit on them, had the obligation to redeem them in gold.

What was the public reaction to the passage of the Federal Reserve Act?

Very few people, including the Congress, actually understood what was happening. However, a few individuals did understand the banker's plot, and were quite vocal in their opposition. Senator Charles Lindbergh, Sr. said, "This Federal Reserve Act establishes the most gigantic monetary trust on earth. When the President signs this bill, the invisible government of the Monetary Powers will be legalized." Lindbergh understood that the power of this "invisible government" was already there. It was just being illegally used. The Federal Reserve Act legalized its operation. Henry Ford, Sr. remarked that if the American people ever understood the rank injustice of the banking system "there would be revolution before morning". President James A. Garfield understood the magnitude of the issue when he said, "Whoever controls the volume of money in any country is absolute master over industry and commerce".

Why doesn't Congress abolish the Federal Reserve Bank?

You would think that the people representing us in Congress would have a basic understanding of something as fundamental as money, but that's not always the case. The majority of the officials who passed the Federal Reserve Act had no understanding of what the bill was for.   David Houston, Woodrow Wilson's secretary of Agriculture, said "The impossible has happened. Today, Tuesday, December 23rd, the currency measure became a law. The President approved it a few minutes after six o'clock in the afternoon. It was passed by a Congress, dominated by the Democrats, two-thirds of whom had been unsound on currency questions, and a majority of whom can scarcely be said to have understood what the measure meant and would accomplish." Not much has changed since 1913. Two-thirds of the Congress didn't understand it then, and two-thirds don't understand it today. Only a handful of leaders have ever raised their voice against the Federal Reserve Banks, and with good reason.

Why do those who do understand the true nature of the Federal Reserve Banking System seem hesitant to speak out?

The folks who understand the problem are either shut up or paid off. Consider the fate of Congressman Louis T. McFadden. In the 1930's he was on the House Banking and Currency Committee, and he put the following into the record: "Mr. Chairman, we have in this country one of the most corrupt institutions the world has ever known. I refer to the Federal Reserve Banks hereinafter called the Fed. The Fed has cheated the Government of these United States, and the people of the United States out of enough money to pay the Nation's debt. The depredations and inequities of the Fed has cost this country enough money to pay the National Debt several times over. This evil institution has impoverished and ruined the people of these United States, has bankrupted itself, and has practically bankrupted our government. It has done this through the defects of the law under which it operates through the maladministration of that law by the Fed, and through the corrupt practices of the money vultures who control it. Some people think that the Federal Reserve Banks are United States Government institutions. They are not Government institutions, they are private monopolies which prey upon the people of these United

States for the benefit of themselves and their foreign customers, foreign and domestic speculators and swindlers, and rich and predatory money lenders. In that dark crew of financial pirates there are those who would cut a man's throat to get a dollar out of his pocket. There are those who send money into States to buy votes to control our legislators, there are those who maintain international propaganda for the purpose of deceiving us into granting a new concession which will permit them to cover up their past misdeeds, and set again in motion their gigantic train of crime. These twelve private credit monopolies were deceitfully and disloyally foisted upon this country by the bankers who came here from Europe, and repaid us our hospitality by undermining our American institutions. Those bankers took money out of this country to finance Japan in a war against Russia. They created a reign of terror in Russia with our money in order to help that war along. They instigated the separate peace between Germany and Russia and thus drove a wedge between the Allies in the World War. They financed Trotsky's passage from New York to Russia so that he might assist in the destruction of the Russian Empire. They fomented and instigated the Russian Revolution, and placed a large fund of American dollars at Trotsky's disposal in one of their branch banks in Sweden, so that through him, Russian homes might be thoroughly broken up and Russian children flung far and wide from their natural protectors. They have since begun breaking up America's homes and the dispersal of American children. Mister Chairman, there should be no partisanship in matters concerning banking and currency affairs in this country, and I do not speak with any. In 1912, the National Monetary Association under the chairmanship of the late Senator Nelson W. Aldridge, made a report and presented a vicious bill called "The National Reserve Association Bill". This bill is usually spoken of as the Aldridge Bill. Senator Aldridge did not write the Aldridge Bill. He was the tool, if not the accomplice, of the European Bankers who for nearly twenty years had been scheming to set up a Central Bank in this country, and who in 1912 had spent and were continuing to spend vast sums of money to accomplish their purpose. We were opposed to the Aldridge plan for a Central Bank. The men who rule the Democratic party then promised the people that if they were returned to power, there would be no central bank established here while they held the reigns of government. Thirteen months later, that promise was broken, and the Wilson Administration, under the tutelage of those sinister Wall Street figures, who stood behind Colonel House, established here in our free country, the worm-eaten monarchical institution of the King's Bank to control us from the top downward, and to shackle us from the cradle to the grave". After five attempts on his life, the outspoken Congressman McFadden was finally assassinated.

Why do many economists seem to endorse the Federal Reserve System?

Economists who truly understand the devastating economic effects of the Federal Reserve System are routinely "rewarded" with high-paying appointments within the Federal Reserve System, or given positions with government-funded institutions. In 1966, Alan Greenspan, the current Fed Chairman, revealed his understanding of the economic blight that the Federal Reserve's fiat currency created in America when he wrote, "The abandonment of the Gold Standard made it possible for the welfare statists to use the banking system as the means to an unlimited expansion of credit. The law of supply and demand is not to be conned. As the supply of money increases relative to the supply of tangible assets in the economy, prices must eventually rise. Thus, the earnings saved by the productive members of the Society lose value in terms of goods. When the economy's books are finally balanced, one finds that this loss in value represents the goods purchased by the Government for welfare or other purposes. In the absence of the Gold Standard, there is no way to protect savings from confiscation through inflation. There is no safe store of value. If there were, the Government would have to make its holding 'illegal', as was done in the case of gold." As can be readily understood, Greenspan, in his current position, has not recently spoken so bluntly about the futility of saving for the future under the Federal Reserve's unbacked zero-reserve monetary system. It is amusing to note that in 1956, Greenspan was an unknown economist, who was then warning "bankers are going to take over the world".

How has the Federal Reserve system created tolerance for "financial irresponsibility" in America?

The system encourages imprudence. Agencies of the Government, banks, savings and loans, and even the people are encouraged to pile on more debt, which is then monetized (turned into money) by the Federal Reserve, causing inflations, defaults, and bankruptcies. The banking industry is the worst offender. Encouraged by the assurance of government bail-outs with Fed-created money, banks have become notorious for fiscal irresponsibility and disastrous lending practices. What other business can you think of where the Government will come in and bail you out when you lose money, and then cover 100 percent of your loses?

What happens if the Fed issues too many Federal Reserve notes?

The Bankers have created a "spillway" for the elimination of excess notes. In 1913, the same year as the Federal Reserve Act was passed, the bankers pushed through our 16th Amendment, authorizing a tax on the income of ordinary citizens. In this way, the banking system could continue to issue volumes of notes into the economy and collect the interest, but not have to worry about a flooded marketplace. The tax removes a portion of the notes in circulation, thereby ensuring that there will always a demand for "new notes". Theoretically, prices would quintuple if all issued Federal Reserve notes were bid against each other at the same time. The income tax was instituted to remove from bidding some of the notes issued and held by the non-bank public. The primary function of all federal taxes and many state taxes today is the same as the income tax: reduce the bidding of the non-bank public by confiscating a portion of circulating Federal Reserve Notes.

Did John F. Kennedy attempt to abolish the Federal Reserve?

Kennedy was one of the few Presidents who had stood up to fight the Federal Reserve Banks. 1963 was a watershed year in our currency's history. We removed the "promise to pay" from the notes and the year after eliminated the silver content from United States Coins, which allowed the further inflation of the monetary system by the Federal Reserve Banks. 1963 was also the year of JFK's Executive Order 11110, which was part of his attempt to reform America's monetary policy. Some historians have publicly speculated that this attempt to revamp our monetary system cost JFK his life. Kennedy apparently knew that by returning to a Constitutional monetary system, and by having The US Treasury issue America's currency (thereby circumventing the Fed), the national debt could be reduced as no interest would need to be paid to the Federal Reserve Banks. On June 4th, 1963, he signed Executive Order 11110, which called for $4,292,893,815.00 in notes to be directly issued through the US Treasury. He also signed a bill changing the backing of one and two-dollar bills from silver to gold, adding strength to the slumping Dollar. James Saxon, Kennedy's Comptroller of the Currency, had been angering the powerful Federal Reserve Board for some time, by encouraging broader lending powers for non-Fed member banks. Saxon had also initiated policies that allowed non-reserve banks to underwrite state and local general obligation bonds again, cutting into the profits of the Federal Reserve Banks. Although a number of the new Kennedy notes were printed and issued, they were quickly withdrawn after Kennedy's untimely demise.

How is the Federal Reserve system set up?

There are three basic parts to the Fed. The Board of Governors is part one. The Reserve banks, (the banks themselves), are part two. This entity known as the Federal Open Market Committee is part three. Practically speaking, they're all intertwined, in that the Board of Governors sets the monetary policy for the entire system. There are seven members, and they're appointed by the

President. The Senate confirms them. They're in office for fourteen years, but they appoint them in staggered terms. That way, theoretically, the President can't "pack" the Federal Reserve. They pick one person as the Chairman, and he holds his position for a four-year period. The Vice Chairman also stays for four years. The President appoints the Chairman and the Vice Chairman.

Does the President ever meet with the Board of Governors?

No, not officially. He contacts them, I'm sure. Control over the system is exercised by the Board and the Board staff.

How does the President make his Fed appointments?

The Federal Reserve Act requires that the President shall have due regard for a fair representation of the financial, agricultural, industrial, and commercial interests and geographical divisions of the country. He only picks bankers, almost exclusively from within the ranks of the New York Banking cliques - agents of J.P. Morgan, Salomon Brothers, Kuhn Loeb, et cetera. After he determines his selection, the President sends the name to Congress for confirmation, like he does for the Cabinet Members.

Is Chairman of the Fed a much-sought-after position?

The Chairman is the single most powerful individual in the system. He controls the staff and he gets to decide quite a bit. It's a great job. It's the ultimate "inside job".

What is the role of the Federal Reserve Banks themselves?

They hold the cash and issue the currency. They actually store the notes and pass them out to the members in their districts.

How many Federal Reserve Banks are there?

There are twelve, and they are in Atlanta, Boston, Chicago,

Cleveland, Dallas, Kansas City, Minneapolis, New York, Philadelphia, San Francisco, St. Louis, and Richmond.

What other functions do these banks serve?

They can cash checks, and you can also cash your Government bonds and make your tax payments. One of their primary functions is to be the fiscal agent of the Government.

What is the corporate structure of the Fed Banks?

Each one is an individual corporation, and each of the corporations has stock which is owned by the commercial banks within its district. For example, the New York Fed, having a higher concentration of commercial banks, has more stockholders than the Kansas City and Cleveland banks. The stock can't be sold or put up as collateral. It's not "corporate stock" like one normally thinks of. No matter how much stock a bank owns, it only gets one vote. If there are seven banks in the Fed Bank's district, and one of them owns a majority of the stock, the other six still get an equal vote. The idea is that by giving all banks an equal vote, no bank can take over the district. The way that they purchase the stock is by putting operating capital into the system. If you open a bank and you start with one thousand dollars, you give the thousand to the Fed. That becomes your operating capital, and they then issue you certificates of stock.

What is the difference between a bank that is part of the Federal Reserve system, and a non-member bank?

There's a huge difference. Non-member banks cannot execute wire transfers, and they can't clear checks "on-line". They're not part of the game. Being a non-member is like being a stock broker without having a seat on the exchange. Sure, you can do business, but it's almost impossible.

How many non-Fed banks are there?

There are several, but the most notable example is the Bank of North Dakota, which was established during the Great Depression. The bank of North Dakota is a State bank, owned by the state. All proceeds from State operations have to be deposited into that bank, not into the Federal Reserve system. This bank makes loans and does all of the things that a member bank would do, including creating money. It has a rich history, and really helps the people in the region. Naturally, we don't hear much about it.

What are Class A, B, and C Directors?

Each of the twelve Federal Reserve Banks is presided over by a Board of nine Directors. Three Class A Directors come from the banks operating within the particular Federal Reserve Banking district. Three Class B Directors are members of the general public, and three Class C Directors are appointed by the National Board of Governors. The Class C Directors are the only ones who can be Chairman and Vice Chairman of the Regional banks. The President and the other Officers can be vetoed by the National Board. In this way, the National Board keeps total control of Federal Reserve Operations over the twelve regions.

Where do the three Class C Directors come from?

They can pick anyone they want, but these directors cannot serve two boards at once. It's a full time job.

What is the function of the Open Market Committee?

The National Board of Governors decides what it's going to do, and the Open Market Committee decides how to do it. For example, if the Board says, "We need interest rates up", then it's up to the Federal Open Market Committee to decide how to get them up. What the Open Market Committee then does is manipulate the money supply by buying and selling Treasury bonds, or foreign bonds, or foreign currency. These covert undertakings are why the Fed is detested by those who really understand its methods.

What other covert manipulations is the Fed guilty of?

One of the tools they have at their disposal is the "currency swap", and it's just evil. Take Mexico, for example, when they got into their monetary crisis. The Federal Reserve Board called up the Mexicans and said, "Look - here's what we'll do. You print fifty-billion dollars' worth of Pesos. Now, we understand that if you take those fifty-billion dollars' worth of Pesos and just dump them into your own economy, it would cause tremendous inflation for you. But because our economy is so much bigger, here's what we'll do instead. You give us the fifty billion dollars' worth of Pesos, and we'll put them in a closet somewhere. In turn, we'll give you fifty-billion Dollars worth of Federal Reserve Notes. You can then take those Dollars and buy Treasury bonds, and use those Bonds as collateral for a loan." It's a great little system. It thereby gives the Mexicans fifty-billion dollars that, in effect, are taken from the taxpayers of the United States. In addition to the inflation this move causes in the United States, we're also stuck with a closet-full of Pesos that we can't do anything with. Ironically, those fifty billion in Pesos "in the closet" will be counted as assets by the Fed, and used to generate more Federal Reserve Notes!

How much is in that "closet"?

The Fed won't tell us that. That's the purpose of doing a currency swap. It's completely secret. It's an internal operation. As they say, it's got nothing to do with us, so they don't tell Congress about it.

Can the amount of US Treasury bonds purchased by Dollars swapped for foreign currency be estimated?

Not really. As with the Mexican example, even though they were forced to purchase bonds, the bonds were purchased on the open market. You can't verify who the end users are of bonds purchased on the open market. Bonds purchased by the Fed routinely are put into various foreign accounts, and those records are not open to inspection or audit. I would estimate that the Fed engages in hundreds of billions of dollars' worth of currency swaps annually. They're doing it with the Germans, the Japanese, the French... they do currency swaps with just about everyone. It's an everyday transaction.

When the Fed engages in bail-outs and currency swaps, does it defend its actions as being in the best interests of the US economy?

That's not the Fed's function. Remember, nowhere in their charter is it stated that they must operate in the best interest of the United States. Remember also that Federal Reserve officials are not elected officials, nor have they sworn oaths of allegiance to the US or to the Constitution. The Fed's only real responsibility is to provide an elastic money supply for the United States. There's been talk about narrowing their mandate and limiting what they can do, but I don't think that will ever happen.

Where is the real power at the Fed?

The reason that the Open Market Committee system was established was to conceal the control of the New York Federal Reserve Bank. The New York Fed is the real head of the monster. Although it's structured to appear that the Federal Reserve Board is the head, it's the New York Fed that calls the shots. It's interesting that when you look over the other eleven Regional Banks, you find "bread-and-butter" America. You can go looking for conspiracies in those eleven banks, and every single person you'll investigate will lead to a dead end. The Directors of the Regional Banks are "Main Street America" businessmen, members of the Kiwanis club - the whole nine yards. It's only when you get into the New York Fed that you find out where the real control is. To my mind, the Federal Reserve Bank of New York has supreme power because the Open Market Committee consists of the National Board of Governors plus five of the twelve Regional Presidents. Now remember, they serve at the pleasure of the Federal Board, but the one exception to that is the President of the New York Fed, who is ALWAYS on the Committee. The other five come from the other twelve banks, and they rotate in. Before they can get an idea of what's going on, they're gone. But the New York Fed is in there, day-in and day-out. As a matter of fact, when the Open Market Committee decides what it's going to do, it's the New York Fed that does it. They don't call up the Cleveland Fed and say, "Okay, buy Treasury bonds". Rather, they call the New York Fed, and the New York Fed does the work. They are the most powerful.

Is the Fed required to release minutes of its meetings?

Prior to the 1970's, the Federal Reserve didn't publicly say anything about its operations. Now, people seem to think that the minutes of the meetings are released, but they're not. It's a "report" of the minutes. The transcripts are actually shredded. The actual transcripts of the meetings have been reduced to a summary, and none of the Freedom of Information rights apply to the Fed's operations.

How does the Fed buy and sell Treasury Bonds?

There are twenty-four primary bond dealers. They are the only twenty-four dealers who can buy and sell Government Bonds. A bond trader from the New York Fed calls one of these dealers and says, "this is the Fed of New York; we're buying thirty-year bonds at XYZ". So, they put in a bid that is calculated to influence the market. If they want to drive interest rates down, they raise bond prices by bidding more than everyone else. If someone tops their bid, they bid again. By buying more bonds they drive interest rates down, and by selling them they push interest rates up.

What happens if the Fed tries to sell their bonds, but there are no buyers?

If they're selling a bunch of thirty-year bonds and nobody wants to buy them, they just print the money! They don't have to attract any money at all. One of the things that Congressman Ron Paul pointed out in his book was that the Federal Government, if it chose to, could just have the Fed print or create all the money the Government needed, and just add it to the money supply. The Government would never need to collect income tax or any other tax. But such a system would be too revealing. Everyone would know that the money supply was increasing, and the dollar would march downward year after year. So this method of buying bonds, which causes interest rates to go down, (even though they really want interest rates to go up), is one of the normal things done at the Fed. They don't always make an obvious move when trying to affect the economy. Their actions are very calculated and covert, rather like Rothschild was just after the Battle of Waterloo. Rothschild's couriers were there in France, and his family was from France, so he learned before anyone else that Napoleon had lost and that Wellington had won. But instead of going to the London Stock Exchange and doing what would have come naturally (which would have been to buy British stocks), he instead went to his post at the London Stock Exchange and started selling British stocks. Everyone saw what he was doing and said, "Oh, Rothschild is selling. This must mean that Wellington lost!" And, naturally, when the other brokers started selling, Rothschild reversed his course and started buying. The Fed plays its own similar games, and it tries to "head-fake" the rest of the market.

Was it coincidence that both the Income Tax Act and the Federal Reserve Act were passed in the same year?

The Federal Reserve System is a system of printing money and withdrawing money. The 16th amendment was passed at the same time as the Federal Reserve Act because the Federal Reserve Act is no good without a heavy progressive income tax. The Income Tax Act creates a legal necessity for everyone to deal in Federal Reserve Notes. Forcing everyone to gather these notes to pay the tax man creates a circle, a pull on the market that otherwise wouldn't be there. In this way, The Fed can create too much money, and have it all sucked right back out of the system in the form of taxation each year.

Was the Federal Reserve Act actually conceived as way to funnel America's wealth to Great Britain?

My contention is that the Federal Reserve Act was put into place in order for the wealth of the United States to be stripped and transferred to Britain so that she would be able to win World War I. The American people would not tolerate a traditional bond issue to aid Britain's cause. There was an election campaign on, and the American people wanted to steer clear of direct involvement. But, behind the scenes, the banking powers in the US wanted to help the British all they could, so they created this wonderful Federal Reserve System with its private notes, calling it the money of the United States, then loaning it to Great Britain, while at the same time circulating it here at home. Then on through the Twenties, when the war was over, all of that money created by the Fed came home to roost. They had effectively doubled the supply of money, and sent half of it to Europe to fight the war and left the other half of it here at home. All through the Roaring Twenties, this excess cash came back and entered the markets. The money in circulation represented twice as many notes as there was gold. The people who understood, the people inside the Fed and the European bankers who knew what had happened, redeemed all of their notes for gold. If you question whether the real purpose of the Federal Reserve was, initially, to provide England with funds to fight World War One, ask this question: Hadn't the English banking interests been trying to institute the Federal Reserve System for the previous 100 years? Clearly they had control of US monetary policy. The Rothschilds had control of the United States' monetary system through the House of Morgan.

Is it possible to predict the Fed's actions?

We have a number of "Fed watchers". They look at the general monetary policy that's set, and they also know that seasonal adjustments take place, wherein the Fed traditionally buys more Bonds than during other times of the year. It's really a process of watching the markets closely, and knowing who the twenty-four Bond agents are. There really isn't any way to know what the Fed will do other than by assessing their general mood though listening to the remarks of the Open Market Committee, or to the remarks of the Fed Chairman and the Governors. Secrecy is the name of their game. They don't want anyone to know their next move.

Does the Fed publish an operating statement?

There is something called the Annual Federal Reserve Report. The December 31, 1991 report shows how much of their money is in land, buildings, construction, and equipment. One number jumps off the page, and that is the value of the Fed's furniture and office equipment - eight hundred and ninety million dollars. They obviously aren't buying their desk lamps at K-Mart!

What is the Federal Reserve "Slush Fund"?

The GAO recently found that the Fed's reported 1994 "expenses" had ballooned to over two billion dollars. This increase was twice as fast as the rate of inflation for the same period. Also uncovered by GAO accountants was a 3.7 billion dollar "surplus account", allegedly established to provide a "cushion" in case the Fed were to lose money in its foreign currencies trades or in its dealings with commercial banks. The Fed's justification for needing such a surplus account is obviously bogus, because in its seventy-nine year history, the Fed has never suffered one penny of loss.

What did Thomas Jefferson say about the ideal monetary system?

This is Jefferson's famous quote: "If our Nation can issue a dollar bond, it can issue a dollar bill. The element that makes the bond good also makes the bill good. The difference between the bond and the bill is that the bond lets money brokers collect twice the amount of the bond plus interest, whereas the bill pays nobody but those who contribute directly in some useful way. The people are basis for Government credit. Why then cannot the people have the benefit of their own credit by receiving non-interest bearing currency instead of bankers receiving the benefit of the people's credit in interest-bearing bonds? It is absurd to say that a country can issue 30 million in bonds and not 30 million in currency. Both are promises to pay, but one fattens the usurers, and the other helps the people."

Why aren't Jefferson's words known by every Congressman and economist?

Real U.S. history is no longer taught in schools. And besides, Thomas Jefferson was a "slave owner". What could he possibly know about administering a free society? That's one of the prevailing attitudes about Jefferson. But there are some who realized Jefferson's brilliance. When Kennedy entertained Kruschev and a group of United Nations officials in the White House dining room, he stood up and made a toast. Kennedy said, "In this room is the greatest concentration of brain power since Thomas Jefferson dined here alone." Jefferson knew that the banking system represented a greater threat to America's freedom than did an armed foreign invasion. The bankers' paper money trickery was nothing new. An old farmer of that day understood money better than a politician does today.

How does the Federal Reserve make money for its owners?

It's not as most people think. The interest the Fed collects on its bond holdings are minuscule compared to the money it can generate from its many unreportable activities. Their biggest profits are all indirect and "off the books". They make it from their perfect information, and from being able to monetize anything they want. As the Federal Reserve, you can monetize a billion-dollar note written by a six-year-old. You can do whatever you want. Here's a perfect example. The Mexicans were getting ready to default on fifty billion dollars' worth of bonds. The primary loser in that scenario would have been Goldman-Sachs, and the secondary loser would have been J.P. Morgan and Co. The Secretary of Treasury, Rubin, (the former vice-chairman of Goldman-Sachs), went before the Congress of the United States and told them that it was of vital national interest that the Mexicans should not default on their loan, and that Congress should give the Mexicans fifty billion dollars. The Congressmen replied that they didn't object to that, but they wanted to learn a little more about what the money would be used for. And with that, the President promptly announced that he didn't actually need Congressional approval for a bailout, as he could just take money out of his Currency Stabilization Fund, and give it to the Mexicans. The money was given to the Mexicans, and the Mexicans promptly gave that money to Citibank, Goldman-Sachs, and every other private Fed-connected bank that bought their worthless bonds. Obviously, it was the cartel who owned the New York Banks and who runs the Fed from behind the scenes who profited from this Fed operation. That was a classic example of how the Fed made billions for its owners.

Who benefits from the Fed's indirect operations?

Its stockholders. The May, 1914 organization chart of the Fed shows that they issued 203,000 shares. National Citibank took 30,000 shares, First National Bank took 15,000 shares, and then those two banks merged in 1955 to create Citibank. With that merger, they held one-quarter of the shares of the New York Fed. The National Bank of Commerce was Paul Warburg's bank. He was the primary architect of the Federal Reserve system, and he took 21,000 shares. Manufacturer's Hanover, Rothschild's bank, took 10,200 shares. Chase took 6,000 and Chemical took 6,000. These six banks owned 40% of the stock of the Fed. As of 1983 they owned 53%, and here's how it breaks down; Citibank owns 15%, Chase Manhattan owns 15%, Morgan Guaranty owns 9%, Manny Hanny owns 7%, and Chemical Bank owns 8%. Citicorp, of course, is the number one bank of the United States now, and

Chemical and Chase just merged, making them number two. Manny Hanny is gone, making J.P. Morgan number three, then First Chicago Trust. By 1982, these same six banks, (Manny Hanny in particular), had loaned two-and-one-half times their net worth to Latin American countries. The proper thing for the Fed to have done would have been to say, "Hey, you loaned two and one-half times your net worth to Brazil, and they didn't pay you. Better luck next time!" But, that's not the way it happened. The Federal Reserve Bank, again "in the national interest", purchased that entire bad debt, with the credit of the American people, as loans, and they called them assets. The obligation to pay the loans went from the Brazilians to the Federal Reserve Bank's Open Market Committee, thereby passing the burden of that debt onto the American taxpayers. Chemical, Citibank, and all the others are riding high today because the Fed assumed all of their debts in the name of the American people.

Logistically, how does the Fed assume a Third-world debt due to a member's bank?

They buy the physical obligation. The Federal Open Market Committee monetizes a particular indenture. They have the ability to monetize anything they want. Breaking it down simply, let's say the sovereign Government of Brazil issues dollar-denominated Treasury Bonds from its Treasury, and the Bank of New York buys those bonds. Ten years later, when those bonds are due, the Federal Government of Brazil cannot make the payment. That's when the Federal Reserve Bank steps in, through the Federal Open Market Committee, and buys those bonds from the Bank of New York. The Bank of New York gets its money back from the Federal Reserve, who now owns the Treasury Bonds issued by Brazil. The Fed carries those bonds on their books as assets, or they pledge them as collateral for other loans, or they swap them with the Japanese. They can do whatever they want with those Brazilian Bonds, as they are now assets. In 1982 they monetized the bonds. Of course, if there's any loss on those bonds, the Fed will deduct that loss from the twenty-two billion that it takes in profit. If the Fed loses all of its yearly profit due to acquiring worthless bonds, it's just chalked up to "the cost of doing business".

Are there other examples of Fed-orchestrated bailouts of other nations?

I could give dozens of examples of similar bail-outs, where the Fed took action without the approval or knowledge of the Congress, allegedly acting in the best interest of the American citizens. The first bailout was in 1914, when the British Government borrowed over one billion dollars from J.P. Morgan and then couldn't pay it. That was the very first purchase by the Federal Reserve Bank of New York. They picked up the billion dollar debt that the British owed to Morgan. They bought the debt of the British Government.

Why doesn't Congress prevent the Fed's bail-outs?

Because the Fed doesn't announce them. That's what an audit would reveal. But because they can't audit the operations of the Federal Open Market Committee, they can't audit Central Bank transactions.

How was the recent "Mexican Bailout" accomplished without Congressional approval?

Under the system our forefathers envisioned, the money would either have to be appropriated by Congress and made available through current taxation, or be bonded in order for this bailout to have occurred. But under the current system, the President was free to simply "create" an additional 20 billion dollars from the "Exchange Stabilization Fund". Although he claimed that twenty billion dollars existed in this fund, this money was not in circulation competing for goods and services. Now it is, and we're just now starting to see the results.

What was the "Haitian Bailout"?

The Haitians owed twenty billion dollars to the New York Banks, but Haiti announced that they wouldn't pay. When the US "liberated" Haiti, the Federal Reserve immediately bought that debt owed to the New York Banks.

Why are New York Banks in the habit of loaning funds to countries who can't repay?

While we were trying to peddle our influence around the world in the late 1970's and early 1980's, we sent forth swarms of bankers out of New York to all the sovereign nations of the world. The Banks knew that anytime a nation failed to make good, the Fed would step in and take care of things. In making their loans, the New York banks didn't even have to consider the credit-worthiness of their potential debtors. The banks even knew that the US could resort to a Fed-backed military invasion to recoup bad debts.

Why was Quebec's threatened secession from Canada potentially devastating to the world's Central Banking system?

If Quebec had withdrawn from Canada, and started its own brand-new debt-free monetary system (not part of the IMF or World Bank), it would have revealed the full extent of the world-wide fraud perpetrated by the major Central Banks around the world. It's imperative that all the industrialized nations work in concert with the Bank of International Settlements, the IMF, and the World Bank. By issuing its own debt-free currency, Quebec would have revealed the extent of the fraud that goes on with the rest of the World's monetary supply. What keeps the system functioning now is the fact that all the world's central banks operate in concert to maintain the appearance of integrity. That is why, relative to each other's currencies, there isn't much perceptible change year-to-year. But if one of the industrialized nations decided to keep its currency fluid, honest, and debt free, then that currency would continually gain strength against the other world currencies. That's the main reason why such a government could not be allowed to exist. With no central bank issuing its currency, an independent and sovereign Quebec would have had more available money to pay to its own citizens, as central bank interest payments would not have to be skimmed off the new nation's money supply.

Does the Bank of England control financial markets today?

Absolutely. The Barings and Rothschilds have been associated with the Bank of England forever. The Rothschilds have always controlled the Bank of England.

Is the premise that "the bankers run the world" really just a myth perpetuated by those who don't really understand the banking system?

The truth is that bankers have indeed conquered entire continents without firing a shot. There is a great quote by the banker Sir Josiah Stamp, former president of the Bank of England. Stamp's listing of directorates filled several pages in "Who's Who". In the late 1920's, during an informal talk to about 150 history, economic, and social science professors at the University of Texas, he said, "Banking was conceived in iniquity and born in sin. The bankers own the world. Take it away from them, but leave them the power to create money and control over that money, and they will create that money right back again. Take this power away from bankers and all great fortunes will disappear, and they ought to disappear, for this then would be a happier, better world to live in. My sons should not object; they are well educated and should be willing to take their place in the business world. But if you want to continue to be slaves to the banker and pay the cost of your own enslavement, then let the bankers continue to create money and control credit. However, as long as government will legalize such things, a man is foolish not to be a banker."

What is "Bretton Woods"?

Bretton Woods refers to a famous meeting of the world's top monetary authorities in New Hampshire during 1944. The agreements reached at Bretton Woods are, in essence, what set the Dollar up as the world standard.

What was decided at Bretton Woods?

The net result of the conference was that things were to be denominated in Dollars. That's how oil came to be denominated in dollars. Ever since that meeting, oil and most other commodities around the world have been quoted in dollars.

Why was it important to the Federal Reserve to have oil denominated in dollars?

By 1944 it became obvious that oil was going to rule the world. The families who had control over the Treasury's printing presses wanted to ensure that there would always be a demand for the dollars they would roll off the presses. By requiring other nations to purchase their oil with American Dollars, those who controlled America's Central bank ensured that there would be a continuing international demand for their Federal Reserve notes. To understand how and why the Fed orchestrated the Bretton Woods agreement, you have to recall that from 1913 to 1933 the Fed said that they were going to print 20 dollars in notes for every ounce of gold. Instead, during that period, they printed 35, maybe 40 dollars for every 20 dollar gold piece. The bulk of those notes went to Great Britain to finance the war. Eventually, during the Roaring 20s, those certificates found their way home when the Europeans began to redeem them for the gold they represented. The Federal Reserve began to realize that it needed someplace else in the world for these repatriated notes to circulate. If those excess dollars could indeed have gone somewhere else, there would have been no "roaring 20's". If there hadn't been a "roaring 20's economy", there wouldn't have been any depression. Had oil been internationally denominated in Dollars during the twenties, the Fed wouldn't have had to crash the stock market to deflate the ballooning domestic money supply, as the excess dollars would never have returned to the United States in the first place.

Why did other foreign countries agree to let oil be priced in dollars?

At the time of the Bretton Woods agreement there was gold backing the American currency, and foreigners knew that their Dollars could be easily redeemed for US gold. The Federal Reserve assured everyone that it would remain that way, but of course the Fed knew better.

How would you rank the hierarchy of players in world banking?

The Bank of England has done a good job in hiding its participation and guidance. Theoretically, you'd have to put the IMF and the World Bank at the top. They are two different entities, closely related. The World Bank is a lending bank in the historical sense. The IMF would be above the World Bank. The IMF is at the very top in the scheme of things.

Who controls the IMF?

The Fabians, apparently, have always pulled the strings. The Fabians are a society, originally a group from England, that believes the United States should be reclaimed by England. The primary force behind the movement was Cecil Rhodes, who died in 1902. He left the majority of his fortune to the Fabian Society. They are up front in admitting they are socialists. They have a slow-moving turtle as their symbol. They advocate that you change society gradually through legislation. They had a stained-glass window made with the names and likenesses of the Fabian Society founders on it. George Bernard Shaw, Sydney Webb, and Cecil Rhodes are pictured on their knees over the slogan "Pray devoutly and hammer stoutly". At the top of the window it says, "Remolded nearer to the Heart's desire".

Are US Government officials connected to the operations of the IMF or World Bank?

Harry Dexter White, the former Secretary of the Treasury, was the IMF's first Executive Director. Robert MacNamara was most recently president of the World Bank.

What is the difference between the IMF and the World Bank?

The World Bank is really the lending arm. They take the spoils and pass them out. The IMF's job is to gather the money.

What is the future of the IMF?

The IMF is going to become the Central Bank of the World. No doubt exists about that. When IMF officials were in the US recently, they warned that the US would have to curtail its debt and get in touch with reality. If the US doesn't do this soon, it will jeopardize its status.

Does the IMF tell the Federal Reserve what to do?

The Federal Reserve pretty much does what the IMF wants it to do and vice versa. It's more cooperation than control.

What are Special Drawing Rights?

Special Drawing Rights (SDRs) are referred to as "paper gold". The IMF uses SDRs extensively. SDRs are bookkeeping entries, which are treated as actual reserves upon which the IMF bases its loans. The IMF derives its "drawing rights" from credit pledged to it by individual countries. When the US "pledges" the IMF a certain sum of money, the US essentially promises the IMF that if this money is needed, the US taxpayers will come up with it. Treating this pledge as though it were an actual lump of cash sitting in its reserve account, the IMF then obtains the right to draw and issue funds, which it loans out to a variety of international entities. It's a gigantic transfer payment scheme, bigger than welfare. For a detailed accounting of the IMF's operations, I would recommend "When Your Bank Fails", by Dennis Turner.

Is the IMF using the American Taxpayer as collateral against its international loans?

Absolutely. But it's doing the same with all the other members of G-7. However, it is Americans who are being asked to guarantee dollars. In its subservient role, the US says to the IMF, "Go ahead and use our taxing power as a base to create 50 billion dollars' worth of money, and if you ever need us to, we'll wring it out of our own citizens". Once the US makes that statement, the IMF can say, "okay, that's an asset. Even though the US hasn't given us any dollars, we can pledge their ability to collect the money in taxes as collateral in a commercial transaction, and turn it into money." Boom! All of a sudden, special drawing rights become dollars. In the past, these IMF dollars have been destined for other countries, but now they are coming home to roost.

What is the total volume of credits that the IMF has to work with?

That figure is not published. It's also uncertain what the current US monetary liability to the IMF is.

Who administers the IMF?

Each member nation sends a delegate.

What is the IMF's purported function?

The IMF is supposed to be the world's bank of last resort. It's a central bank to the world's banks.

How does the IMF operate as a bank of last resort?

In the 1980's there was a huge problem with various "banana republic debts". None of these 3rd World republics could pay their debts by 1982. Kissinger wrote a piece on NAFTA in 1993, and he revealed a good deal about IMF operations at the time. To prevent a series of massive defaults, it was agreed that the IMF would become final guarantor for Citibank. The IMF would rewrite all the bad loans that Citibank had made to these third-world countries, and roll the loans over into the IMF, by means of what are known as "currency swaps". The Fed obtained IMF loans for the various debtor banks... to prevent the US creditor banks from going belly-up, as they were in big trouble.

Why did US banks loan so many billions to questionable 3rd World activities?

The concept is that people can go broke, but that Governments will never go broke. Why not? Because the IMF and the Lending country central bank will always work out a scheme to get funds to the defaulting country so their payments will be met. With this in mind, all through the 70's, Citibank, Chase Manhattan, and the other big players were urged by our Central Bank to get out into the World to loan money to other nations. Manufacturers Hanovers loaned 2.5 times its net worth just to Latin American countries. But by the early 1980s, it became obvious that none of the debtor nations were ever going to pay. Rather than let their own banks go bust, the Fed arranged a loan from the IMF to Mexico. And the Mexicans paid off the private US banks.

Who paid off the IMF?

The Mexicans did. The Mexican banks paid off the American banks, and thereby they owed money to the IMF. They taxed the hell out of the population to pay. Meanwhile, we started giving them foreign aid, something like 35 billion dollars during the first three years of Reagan's Presidency... quietly. The American taxpayers never heard about this. The IMF gave Mexico 35 billion because Mexico owed 30 billion to three New York Bankers, which was due right away. The deal was pay 30 billion, and roll over 30 billion. Oddly enough, it was later revealed that the Mexicans gave at least 100 million dollars of the bail-out money to Castro.

What are "currency swaps'?

It's a maneuver that Central Banks use to loan funds to other Central Banks that are in trouble, without actually going through the bother of Congressional hearings and appropriations. The Fed will print up 600 billion dollars, and exchange those dollars with 600 billion dollars' worth of Pesos. These swaps serve in essence as emergency loans. If the Fed decides to swap US currency for a Third World currency, it doesn't have to make a public recording of its resulting trading loss until the end of the quarter, and usually by that time it is able to persuade the IMF to cover the loss. Foreign assistance of this nature is done by the Fed as discreetly as possible

What is a "debt swap"?

Similar to a currency swap, only more permanent, where bonds are traded instead of notes. The maneuver allows the receiving country to use the U.S. bonds as collateral for a loan.

Why are currency swaps and debt swaps done discreetly?

The Central Banks know that the swaps aren't perceived as inflationary by the general market. They give the illusion of a legitimate reserve, based upon which the participating Central Banks can issue more currency. In 1988, Mexico created 500 million dollars worth of pesos, and gave it to the Federal Reserve in exchange for 500 million US Dollars. Mexico then used those dollars to purchase T-bonds, which will come due in 2018, and be worth 3.7 billion. The Mexicans are using the 3.7 billion dollar value of the US bonds it holds as a leverage for creating tens of billions of dollars of their own currency, thereby legitimizing its worth.

Who sets the policy for the World Banks & IMF?

Many point to the Trilateral Commission, or the Masons, et cetera, but my research has lead to the Fabians. That's where I believe the real decisions are made in the world. The Bretton Woods conference was pretty much dominated by members of the Fabians. Their philosophy is summed up by the graphics and text appearing on their Fabian Window. Under the line "Dear

Love, remolded nearer to the heart's desire", the scene depicts Shaw and Webb hammering at the earth, remolding it. Also depicted are the humble masses, kneeling and worshiping on a stack of texts which advance the socialist doctrine. Thumbing his nose at the subservient masses is H.G. Wells. It was Wells that eventually left the group, calling them "the New Machiavellians". Perhaps the most telling part of the window is their "Fabian Crest", a wolf clad in sheep's clothing. This secret clique of socialists had the huge financial empire of Cecil Rhodes with which to quietly establish behind the scenes dominance. These Fabians were the first to express the desire for a one-world, socialist-dominated planet.

How did the Fabians influence monetary events in the 20th Century?

They were the ones who called for the Bretton Woods meeting in 1944. The pretense was, "hey, we're ending a war here, let's get together and decide on where the World's going to go. What are we going to do?" They set up the foundation for the world bank and IMF, put a gold exchange standard in place, then worked out how gold was going to be eliminated in international trade, and finally determined what was going to replace it. Effectively, they got together and said "The war's over and we own the world now. Let's divide it up".

How did the Fabians initiate the Bretton Woods meeting?

John Maynard Keynes was the monetary expert pushing the economic principles, and Harry Dexter White arranged the meeting. White was Assistant Secretary of the Treasury at the time, and was connected to J.P. Morgan. There is evidence that Morgan was pulling White's strings, and Morgan was an agent for the Rothschilds in the US. So we actually have the Rothschilds controlling Morgan controlling Assistant Secretary White. And remember, it was old man Rothschild who declared he didn't care who made the laws, as long as he and his family could print the money.

What was John Maynard Keynes' role at the Bretton Woods Convention?

Keynes' economic pronouncements were probably the primary moving force behind getting all the parties to the table. Once everyone bought into his theories, it was possible to have a structured system and financial order with which the top clique could financially rule the world. Keynes said, "you don't need gold; it's a barbarous relic - the idea of needing gold behind money was ridiculous". He's credited as the originator of the theory, the first to state it publicly.

Was Keynes in the employ of the top banking families?

Unquestionably yes, in my opinion. His employers had to be the people whose interest it was to eliminate gold as the world's monetary standard. These of course were the people who were running the Federal Reserve Banks. They had put themselves into a hole by issuing these notes, and by having lied about those notes being backed by gold. The only thing that was stopping them from performing their wizardry was the fact that gold was the denominator. If it wasn't, then they could really go wild. So I wouldn't doubt that the Rothschild clique was behind the concept, and had pushed Keynes and his theory to the forefront. He was the perfect front man. And Harry Dexter White was the front man for their interests in the US.

What other members of the Fabian Society have had influence over contemporary economics and politics?

Colonel Edward Mandell House was a Fabian. House was Chief Advisor for Woodrow Wilson, and many say he was Wilson's mentor. House convinced Wilson to sign the Federal Reserve Act into law. There was another very prominent Fabian, whom I thought was a great President, but who was linked to Fabian ideas. He was John Kennedy. He attended the Fabian London School of Economics for two years while his father was the Ambassador to England. I have a Kennedy speech from

September of 1963 inwhich JFK was addressing finance ministers and central bank governors. "Everybody" was there. One hundred countries were represented for the annual meeting of the IMF. Kennedy said, "Twenty years ago, when the architect of these institutions (the IMF) met to design an international banking structure, the economic life of the world was polarized in an overwhelming and alarming measure on the United States. Sixty percent of the gold reserves of the world were here in the United States, and there was a need for redistribution of the financial resources of the world." From those words it's unmistakably clear that one of our most cherished Presidents was solidly in agreement with the cornerstone of the Fabian doctrine. The entire situation in which the population of the industrialized nations find themselves today has all come about, not by chance, but by conscious and deliberate long term planning and execution.

What other prominent former US officials were connected to the Fabian movement?

We can go back to the founding of the Council on Foreign Relations. One of its founders was Dulles, General Eisenhower's man. John Foster Dulles believed in diluting the sovereignty of all the nations in the world, especially the US. He made the first call for a one-world currency in 1940. His brother, Alan, became director of the CIA. John Foster was Secretary of State. Here's his quote from the New York Times, October 28, 1939: "Some dilution or leveling-off of the Sovereignty system as it prevails in the world today must take place, to the immediate disadvantage of those nations which now possess the preponderance of power. The establishment of a common money would deprive our government of exclusive control over a national money. The United States must be prepared to make a sacrifice, afterwards, in setting up a world political economic order which would level off inequality in economic opportunities respective to nations".

Do private vested interests currently influence the American economy via their influence over Government programs?

What's interesting to take note of are the names prominently involved in today's pharmaceutical industry - names like the Rockefeller Foundation, the Von Swearinger Family, the Chase Banking family, The Mellon Group, the Paynes and the Aldriches, the Whitneys, the Morgans and their descendants, and the group at Dillon-Reid and Brown Brothers Harriman. These families have been influencing America's economic policy forever, and getting fantastically rich in the process. Now who owns twelve of the fourteen largest drug companies of the world? Is it any wonder that Medicaid payments are so high? The average senior citizen takes several hundred dollars' worth of prescription medicine each month, most of it unnecessarily. Who pays for these drugs? American taxpayers. Who benefits? The drug companies, with their outrageous mark-ups. We not only find flagrant profiteering via social programs in the area of drugs, but it is also prevalent with the agricultural fraud at the Agriculture Department, and the hawking of licenses with the Federal Communications Commission, and the use of the dozens of Federal alphabet soup agencies to crush competition. The Justice department is swarming all over Microsoft. Why? Because the people who own Microsoft are not the people in Government. Remember the saccharin scare? Ronald Reagan took office, and as soon as the administration changed, saccharin was found to be cancer-causing in laboratory rats. Some foundation discovered this fact, undoubtedly with a grant. What they found, really, was that if you remove everything from a rat's diet except saccharin, then it's going to get cancer. They banned saccharin out-right as an artificial sweetener, and aspartame, amazingly, just happened to be ready and waiting to go. Look at who owns the company which makes aspartame. Who is Archer Daniels Midland? Who is Cargill International? How could they, by sheer luck and co-incidence, profit so handsomely by a Government agency's action of banning their main competitor from the marketplace while that same agency gives their own artificial additive the fastest green-light in FDA history?

In addition to establishing a one-world currency, what other means of control are the "New Worlders" implementing?

Part of the control mechanism espoused by the CFR-Trilateralist connection deals with environmental control. One of the ideas recently advanced is that the American people would accept a certain amount of encroachment on their freedoms in the name of a war to protect the environment. Bear that in mind as you hear about all of this legislation concerning polluters. A "war" has been publicly "declared" on the big polluters. It's ironic that, despite this war, the big manufacturers of toxic chemicals have no problem getting formaldehyde and toxic preservative agents into your home via their laundry soaps and cleaning products. The actual regulations that are originated by these environmental agencies are used to prevent Americans from building a house in their yard, or planting cabbage out in their field, and, in general, are aimed at prohibiting any activity potentially competitive to the privileged elite. The policies and actions of the EPA are sold to Americans in the name of environmental protection, but these programs are routinely used as weapons against competitors and political enemies.

Has the Orwellian tale of Big Brother become a reality?

Orwell was one of the original Fabians. He knew their intent and motives. What Orwell was actually doing through his "fiction" was leaking their plans. That's why he was so accurate. He had inside information. He studied the Fabians' program for social restructuring. Some would say that the concept of a planned, steady, long-term global conquest is pure fantasy. But if we can accept the fact that a group of men could get together in a smoke-filled room and plot how to take over a company, why can't we accept that a group would get together and plot how to take over a country or economy? I suggest that "social engineering" began around George Orwell's time, and the society in which we live today represents the product of that social engineering. Through the destruction of the family unit and through the usurpation of our monetary system, we have been converted into a socialistic nation without a shot being fired. It was a brilliant strategy.

Was the House of Rothschild the true force behind the establishment of the Federal Reserve?

The Rothschild banking empire clearly was the motivating force behind the establishment of Central Banking in America. Not many realize how powerful the Rothschild empire was, and is today. The House of Rothschild was much more powerful than any financial empire in history, and it wielded tremendous global influence. It answered neither to the world's Governments nor to the people. Its influence was always exercised secretly. The Rothschilds were official bankers for the countries of France, England, Austria, Belgium, Spain, Portugal, Brazil and many of the various German states. They were quite secretive about their political involvements, and were never seen engaging in open public debates on important economic issues. Even so, they were able to control events through granting or withholding loans to highly placed persons, businesses, and governments. The Rothschilds gave Cecil Rhodes, the Fabian's financier, control over the diamond fields of South Africa, and today they still control those same diamond fields through their De Beers affiliate.

Did any of the lobbyists for the Federal Reserve Act acknowledge their affiliation to the Rothschild empire?

No. As a matter of fact, it was a secret throughout most of Morgan's life. No one ever suspected that J.P. Morgan was a Rothschild agent. Of those original Jekyll Island participants, you had Nelson Aldrich, who was tied to J.P. Morgan. Then you had Frank Vanderlip, who was Citibank's president at the time, and he was tied to Kuhn-Loeb (Kuhn-Loeb being Rothschild's agent in North America). Rothschild never came to New York and said, "this will be a Rothschild program". Instead, they backed J.P. Morgan or his father, Junius Morgan and Kuhn-Loeb. Through Morgan and Kuhn-Loeb, Rothschild controlled the New York money markets. Henry Davison was also present, and he was J.P. Morgan's partner. Charles Norton was also J.P. Morgan's partner. Benjamin Strong was the head of Banker's

Trust, and that was a J.P. Morgan arm. Paul Warburg was a partner in Kuhn- Loeb. Between Kuhn Loeb and J.P. Morgan and Co, the Rothschild's interests dominated the planning for the Federal Reserve.

Who runs the Rothschild empire today?

Phillipe. He's headquartered in France. He is the richest man on the planet. You don't hear much about him. You never see him or read anything about him. They hate that limelight. People consider him to be just a very private individual who's living on the family's wealth. Actually, he prefers to operate wine and champagne vineyards. I personally believe that others have taken over all of the day-to-day financial and social planning work for the Rothschilds. The Rothchilds don't have to be directly involved anymore. They stay well above the fray.

Who is "running the world"?

My investigation shows it's the Fabians. If I had to point my finger somewhere, that's where I would point, at the Fabians. Fabians believe that Britain and the United States should be reunited under a socialist government. The Fabians are British Socialists and "One-Worlders". Remember that President Bill Clinton was a Rhodes Scholar, and was oriented to the Fabian program.

Can the National Debt ever be repaid?

The Debt can never be repaid, because the money needed to pay the interest is never created. We have a "Debt Money System", and it can never work and be prosperous for anyone except those who issue the money. The Debt Money System has been used to debauch the currencies of nearly every country, transferring the national wealth to the individuals who own the stock of the issuing bank. This results in the transfer of a nation's assets through the repayment of the Debt with the original Gold and Silver reserves upon which the money system was first based.

Could the US ever repudiate its National Debt?

Anyone who thinks that the United States Government could not repudiate its Debt should simply look at a Silver Certificate. The silver dollars that are called for on the Silver Certificate are not there for you in the United States Treasury, as promised by this note. Although it appears to be an iron-clad guarantee, it's absolutely worthless in terms of metal specified on the note's face.

How will our National Debt be paid?

The Fed will reduce the value of the Dollar so that the debt is repaid with less valuable money.

What does our National Debt consist of?

The majority of the money in this nation is not in the form of cash or in demand deposits at the bank, but is in the form of long-term Treasury obligations that have anywhere from an eighteen-month to a thirty-year maturity. These obligations make up what we call the National Debt. The majority of these bonds are held by over 170 separate trust funds maintained by the Government.

Could Congress pass a bill that would simply cancel our National Debt?

It's an attractive idea, but we can't really do that. Over the years, the US Government has convinced "we the people", through various maneuvers, to establish trust funds. There are many different trust funds that "we the people" have established for various things, such as fixing our roads and building new airports. We also have our Medicaid trust fund, and our Social Security trust fund, and our Government Employees retirement funds. We Americans have put almost three trillion dollars of hard-earned money into these trust funds, and I'm not talking about imaginary money, because each week we see the deductions coming out of our paychecks from the current money we earn. But what many people don't realize is that our weekly trust fund "contributions" are remitted right into a big bucket. The cash is not segregated into the specific trust funds. The Government takes all the cash that pours into our various trust funds every day, and then replaces that money with IOUs called Treasury bonds. As a result, three trillion dollars of the National debt is owed to trust funds that are earmarked for various things. Take, for example, the Highway Trust fund. Supposedly, there are billions of dollars in it. So, why are our roads in such terrible condition? Because the principal is never used to repair the roads - only the interest. To spend the principal would create additional inflation and would not be politically viable. That's why some people think this whole national debt is a mirage... because these 170 trust funds don't seem to have any money in them. They are filled with IOUs.

Why couldn't the Government print up 5 trillion dollars in cash and then just pay off the debt?

The inflationary implications of suddenly introducing that much cash into the economy would be devastating, to say the least. Persons who have carefully been saving money over the years would instantly be reduced to paupers, as the purchasing power of funds in their bank accounts would be cut by a factor of ten. A far better idea would be to issue 500 billion dollars worth of "United States Notes" to replace our current Federal Reserve Notes. That alone would save about 45 billion dollars per year in interest. This prudent action can be taken without affecting any current spending programs.

Can we keep rolling over the National Debt indefinitely?

The annual interest payment will tell the whole story. When you get to where you're spending 60 or 70 percent of the Nation's total income in interest payments, that's the real telling point. Taxes are about as high as they can go. If politicians began talking about raising taxes, they'd be pilloried. The people feel they are taxed to their limit. Every tax dollar west of the Mississippi is currently necessary just to pay the interest on the Debt.

Some think that budget cuts will free up enough extra cash with which to service the Debt. But when the entitlement spending plus interest payments consume 88 cents out of every dollar taken in, what is there left to cut? We've reached the point where we have a very dangerous combination of events. We financed the entire Vietnam war with bonds, and they are coming due right now. Eighty percent of our total debt is coming due before 2000. What's to prevent us from rolling the Debt over? The answer is the huge interest payment. It's getting bigger every day.

Is a complete financial collapse unavoidable?

I'm not one who predicts a complete financial collapse, although there is that possibility. What I see is a steady hyperinflation over the next seven years, so we'll all be talking about two dollar candy bars, three dollar per gallon gas, and one hundred thousand dollar cars like it was nothing unusual.

If an economic collapse does occur, will there be any warning signs?

Before you see a collapse, you will see an inflation. That's the thing I think most "gold bugs" missed. You must have an inflationary cycle before a collapse. All of the writers who predicted collapse in the early 80's never expected that the US Government would allow us to go this far before inflating the currency.

Given the size of the US debt, and the virtual impossibility of ever paying it off, why hasn't the Dollar totally collapsed?

Some people miss this important factor in the equation: The dollar is given a tremendous boost because it is the currency of choice for foreign nations. Foreign nationals would rather store their wealth in 100 dollar bills than in their own local currency because of the difference in the rates of inflation. Some countries have annual inflation rates of 20, 30, even 100 percent. It makes sense for them to hold dollars. This results in increased strength for the Dollar. It gives demand to it. Additionally, you have entire foreign economies pricing their goods in dollars - oil, for example. Anyone in the world who wants oil has to convert their own currency into dollars, thereby creating demand. My fear is that if the Dollar gets any weaker the nations of the world might decide not to hold their reserves in dollars, then send those dollars back to the United States. This one action alone could destroy our economy overnight.

To get the Nation out of debt, could the Government sell the United States' gold reserves?

The gold reserves of the nation are pledged against the Federal Reserve Note issue. We can't sell the gold reserve, because it's pledged. The gold technically doesn't even belong to the United States. It belongs to the privately-owned Federal Reserve Banks.

How much money is stored in the US Treasury?

The Treasury doesn't store any money, nor do the commercial banks. The money is in the Federal Reserve Banking System. The Federal Reserve Banks control the wealth of the world. Until we really understand that, and how the Federal Reserve system functions, there's no hope for getting our monetary house in order.

How stable is our current banking system?

Due to the present electronic nature of currency, should any event occur in the United States to shake the confidence of the global investment community, a financial collapse in America would occur so suddenly that the lifetime savings of 95% of all Americans would evaporate in one or two minutes. Despite the fact that our politicians assure us that they are in control of the Debt situation, America is in fact swimming steadily toward the brink of financial disaster. What troubles me is that most Americans have their money tied up in these IOU's, or they're giving their money to a fund, to invest in whatever the fund sees fit. The amount of American assets pouring into mutual funds is rising at a record pace right along with the Dow. Until people realize that our present system is a precariously balanced house of cards, they won't take any steps to protect themselves. The vast majority of Americans' investment holdings are paper-based, and too many people are chasing those paper profits.

What events could trigger a collapse?

The recent debt ceiling increase, if it would have been proposed as a clean increase to 5.5 trillion, would have been enough to set the world on its ear. But by going through the recent machinations, we were able to wind up with an increase of 500 billion dollars, and no one is concerned. In fact, everyone is breathing a sigh of relief that we raised it to 5.5 trillion. It won't be long until we hit this new ceiling, and international investors might get very uneasy when they see that America has to borrow another half trillion to again postpone a default. In fact, the Republican plan for balancing the budget calls for allowing the debt to soar over seven trillion dollars by 2002. Any lack of confidence from foreign quarters could trigger a bond sell off which would decimate the Dollar's value.

What are the economic consequences when a Government borrows more and more to avoid default?

They are inflationary. Effectively, what the Congress is saying is "we want to raise the debt ceiling to 5.5 trillion dollars, then we're going to print a half trillion dollars worth of bonds, and then the Federal Reserve, if necessary, will create a half trillion dollars in order to buy those bonds." For the working American, there will be no shortage of money. There is no "crowding-out" effect. In fact, there's actually an increase in the supply of money. But the American people will not be told that by increasing the money supply 10 percent, you're going to decrease the value of the dollars in their wallets by 10 percent. The inflation won't happen overnight. By the time the effects are felt, the people who are responsible will be retired, spending their excess campaign contributions and living on their generous government pensions.

Based on the Government's current Debt obligations, what is America's short-term financial outlook?

Dismal. Ross Perot pointed out in the campaign of 1992 that seventy percent of our total debt was due and payable within five years. The number of Treasury Bond auctions scheduled for 1996 is absolutely staggering. The announcers on the Financial News channels are amazed at the quantity of the debt being brought to market. Never before in the history of this Republic has this quantity of debt been brought to the market, and it's going to affect one of two things. Either the Federal Government will crowd out all the private borrowers, thereby driving interest rates up, which in an election year is not going to happen, or they will create whatever supply of money is necessary to pay all this impending debt. All that freshly-created money will go into stocks, it will go into gold, it will go into real estate, and it will seem to most Americans that there is no problem with the economy whatsoever. In fact, there will be quite a general euphoria. There will be a roaring summer economy, a roaring economy into the election, a roaring Dow, jobs and money everywhere, and plenty of money to borrow with low interest rates. It's easy to see why many people believe the Federal Reserve Bank can control elections.

What would happen if the United States went into default on its interest payments?

Loss of sovereignty. Some people suggest that we should just let the whole system crash and burn, then rebuild it from the ashes. But the US is not operating in a vacuum. They think that after a US default, the US will maintain jurisdiction over the problem. But the fact is, if the Federal Government defaults on its Treasury's obligations, it will be hauled before an international court, and foreclosed upon.

How would creditors foreclose on the US?

In the same way one would foreclose on any of the other nations which spend more than they take in. You simply get a judgement against the debtor who doesn't pay. In the case of an international issue, that jurisdiction falls under the World Trade Organization, right in the Hague. So you can't assume you can default on the National Debt and then not be held accountable.

How would such a foreclosure be administered?

What would actually occur is that the "taxing authority" would pass from the Congress to the bailing-out institution, like the International Monetary Fund, or perhaps the World Bank. The way that a bail-out would occur would be that a third party would create "World Currency Units", or "North American Currency Units", and they would offer an exchange of these things, "dollar for dollar". If you had a dollar on deposit in the banking system, they would exchange it for one of these new currency units, and then the power of taxation would pass to this new organization, similar to the Mexican "bail out". Mexico has been made to funnel all of its oil dollars through the New York Federal Reserve Bank in order to get the cash. The US would be forced to do the same thing. We would be forced to funnel all of our tax revenues either through the World Bank, the Bank of International Settlements, or another global clearinghouse of that kind.

Would a US default bring us closer to a one-world Government?

A default would mean one giant leap toward a one-world consolidation. There are people who are convinced that this Nation is hell-bent toward a one-world government, and if you believe that, then you should pay particular attention to what would happen in the case of a US default. It would play right into that scenario. Certainly, what you need in order to establish a one-world government is a one-world currency and the elimination of trade borders.

What would be the role of the UN in the event of a US default?

In the event of a default, we would not rise up from the ashes as a free Republic with our own monetary autonomy. In the court of international law, we would be a debtor nation with a judgement against us, and the creditors could move to enforce those actions, up to and including UN sanctions. When we were brought into the UN, it was all done "tongue in cheek" so to speak. We nudged each other and said, "Yes, we'll abide by their decisions, but if we don't like what they're doing, we'll veto it." And that's why the American People bought membership in that body.   But now, with the advent of the World Trade Organization, and the consequential loss of American Sovereignty, who will the sanctions be put against?

How would the market behave on the day of a US Default?

The door would slam shut. All these people who have mutual funds, who seem to think you can get in and out very easily, have never tried to get out during a falling market. Everyone in a mutual fund would immediately see their asset value evaporate. If they somehow managed to get a sell order through, they'd be lucky to come away with half of their money. Effectively, you'll be able to wipe out a big pile of existing monetary value, spreading the losses out over a wide base. There are one or two hundred major mutual funds, and they represent the capital of millions of investors. Any sudden drop in market values would catch all of them in one big net. The "break", as this precipitous drop in market values is called, would start in Tokyo. In New York, while everyone in America slept, officials would already know that the "break" was happening. You'd wake up in the morning and the financial markets would be in chaos, the long bond would have tanked 2, 3, maybe 4 points overnight, and gold would have shot up in multiples of its trading range.

How high would gold climb on the day of default?

Trading limits would go into effect, in that we don't trade gold anymore. The physical possession gold market would shut down instantly, since the futures market (derivatives market) would have reached its limit for the day and would have stopped trading, so the "official price" of gold would be bogus, and no one retaining physical possession of gold would sell at those levels. So, what you'd see would be the collapse of the gold derivatives market, much as the tin market collapsed. Presently, there is three and one-half times the total supply of gold on the planet today being risked right now in the derivatives market. Therefore, in order to settle every trade in the derivatives market, you'd need three and one-half times the total amount of gold currently above ground!

What would UN sanctions be in the event we default on interest payments?

They can put a trade embargo on us to prevent us from selling products overseas, or in the event that products do get through, they can move to seize whatever monies are due. The UN can legally take action regarding sanctions, especially now that the WTO, NAFTA and GATT agreements are in place. We are now just another member state. And if we fall into a rough position, don't expect the same kindness that we gave to other nations. "Don't worry Germany, we're going to forgive your 50 billion dollar debt... Don't worry about it, Egypt and Israel, you don't owe us any more money." We will not be treated with such kid gloves. You have to consider where the United States has gone in the last forty years. We've gone from the biggest creditor nation, and therefore the one least likely to be pushed around, to the biggest debtor nation, and now the one most likely to be pushed around. No one's going to give us an outstretched hand without some serious strings attached.

If the US went into default, what role would our US military play?

While some assume that the US might rebel against sanctions imposed by international bodies, it seems likely that our military, falling under international law, would more likely be the enforcers of UN sanctions, rather than the protectors of the people.

Could the US tell its creditors to "go take a hike"?

The first thing to realize, if the US repudiated its debt, is that the Social Security Trust fund would be broke. The number one item in Social Security Trust Funds are Treasury Bonds. If the Government defaults on its debt, then Social Security collapses immediately. Not five years or seven years from now, but tomorrow. And all the other trust funds would also be affected. The Civil Service Employee Pensions would be gone. The Federal Deposit Insurance Corporation would be gone. There are 170 different funds with three trillion dollars in bonds, all of it United States debt. Three trillion would be wiped out of the money supply, and if the Government defaulted, then, technically, that money would no longer exist! If you wiped three trillion out of the money supply, a depression would ensue that would rock the foundations of this nation. A default would be the worst thing to have ever happened in financial history.

Are Federal Reserve Notes "sound money"?

An individual will always be able to trade his labor for produce. An individual can be likewise assured that he will be able to trade gold and silver for produce. But can we be certain that we'll always be able to trade Federal Reserve Notes, pieces of paper backed by nothing tangible, for produce?

Can wealth be safely stored in Federal Reserve Notes?

We must realize that the nature of our zero reserve banking system causes a continual depreciation of one's wealth as represented by Federal Reserve Notes. Since the Federal Reserve took control of regulating the value of money, the dollar has fallen by more than 80 percent.

What factors contributed to the stock market's incredible surge in the first half of 1996?

The reason for the run-up in the stock market was because of all the "fresh money" that came into the market as the result of

Treasury Secretary Rubin's maneuvers, when he took money from the civil servant's trust funds (M-3), and converted it into instant money, "M-1".

Was he legally authorized to do that?

As the Secretary of the Treasury his actions were proper and prudent. He acted to save the Treasury of the United States from default. But as the trustee of the Government Employees trust fund, he breached his fiduciary responsibility. He allowed the fund to be effectively looted. He took an IOU from a deadbeat.

Are bonds a better vehicle for storing wealth than Federal Reserve Notes?

If you're like most Americans, your wealth is denominated in Federal Reserve Notes. You may have either a money market account, corporate bonds, municipal bonds, or other Government obligations, and therefore consider yourself well-diversified. However, any underlying instability in the Federal Reserve Note wreaks havoc in returns and yields with all Federal Reserve Note-denominated vehicles.

Why are Federal Reserve Notes a poor vehicle for wealth preservation?

As you exchange your goods, services, and excess capital for Federal Reserve Notes, and you thereby build up accounts of them, you're allowing an invisible force to reduce the value of your wealth. It's an additional tax, actually, and it's the result of excess Government spending. If one estimates that actual inflation has averaged about five percent per annum over the last fifteen years, this means that every dollar saved in 1980 has lost more than one-half its purchasing power. As more and more fiat currency is printed, the value of existing savings is reduced. One often hears the familiar phrase, "a dollar isn't what it used to be". One never hears anybody saying "a gallon isn't what it used to be"!

How has the value of the Dollar changed over the past thirty years?

In 1967 the average three-bedroom home sold for about $14,000. A top-of-the-line car could be purchased for around $3,000. A 1799 ten dollar gold piece could have been purchased for about $300. Today, that house is worth $150,000. The car is selling for $30,000... a ten-fold increase. The gold coin is trading at about $5,000, a fifteen-fold increase. What this reflects is not really a scarcity of houses, cars, and gold coins, but the erosion of the value of the Federal Reserve Notes used to purchase these items.

What is a "401-K"?

A 401-K is a financial vehicle, and what's inside the 401-K makes the difference. You can put gold coins, stocks, or bonds in your 401-K. If you have a 401-K, and it contains bonds, then I would urge you to sell them as fast as you can. At least buy stocks, or gold and silver coin.

What are "derivatives'?

Derivatives are options. Derivatives take their value not from the item itself, but from the right to trade that item. For example, if I said, "I'm going to give you the right to buy 100 ounces of gold from me in November at a price of 425 dollars per ounce", even though I don't have the gold, and even if you have no intention of buying the gold, we can gamble on the price of gold. It's gambling on scenarios. It's not having physical possession of the item, but rather, having a contract that derives its value from the ability to buy that item. Derivatives can be bought on bonds, on stocks, on gold, on commodities of all types. That's what got the Treasurer of Orange County in trouble recently, because he figured that interest rates were going to fall, and he bought the option, that is, the right or the obligation to buy a certain number of bonds at a certain date in the future, and when that date arrived, the bonds were worth far less than the price he had to pay. That's how he lost all that money.

How do derivatives work in the gold market?

There are two primary methods for trading derivatives in the gold market. The first way is a contract which requires no premium payment, but requires an obligation to buy gold at a set price in the future. The second derivative is less risky, and involves paying a premium for the option to buy gold at a fixed price at some point in the future. The primary difference between the two is that the contract compels performance, while the option does not.

How did the derivatives market gain so much popularity?

The Federal Reserve Bank's Open Market Committee encourages the use of derivatives, because they use them to shelter their financial maneuvers. If the Open Market Committee decides that interest rates need to go down, and in order to make them go down, they should buy bonds (thereby driving up the price and driving down the yield), they sell or buy derivatives of bonds. They don't have to actually "load up" on the bonds themselves. They want to be able to affect the market by buying or selling "options". And the same is true with gold. The entire derivatives market has developed in such a way as to let the "big boys" manipulate the markets so that the average guy cannot figure out what's going on.

How can the Federal Reserve influence gold prices through the derivatives market?

Let's assume that everyone panics tomorrow and starts rushing out to buy gold. Normally, the price of gold would skyrocket. But if the Federal Reserve Banks can sell contracts on gold, thereby meeting the demand and filling the supply, they will cause the price to remain stable, or at least not jump so quickly. They then have the whole time that derivative or that option runs to "unwind their position". So, instead of the price of gold jumping 100 dollars overnight, it rises 100 dollars over three months, and nobody figures out what's going on. Anyone who holds any admiration for the Federal Reserve probably holds it for this reason: they are the best jugglers you'll ever see.

What can the average person do to protect himself from the manueverings of the big financial players?

The best thing they can do is to start moving a portion of their wealth into the tangibles market. Find a broker that deals in lawfully issued gold and silver coin, and then buy some. Familiarize yourself with the market. In the period from 1977 to 1980, when inflation was raging, we saw the average gold coin increase in value by almost 1,000 percent. Indeed, the best advice is to slowly move into tangibles such as coins. When the market gets in trouble, or paper-based assets suddenly lose value, remember the Golden Rule: He who has the gold makes the rules. In a system where there's financial chaos everywhere, and people are losing their shirts in stocks, bonds, and other paper-type investments, tangibles shine. And the person who has those tangibles will be able to swoop in and take advantage of bargains. I recall in 1980 entire houses changing hands for $2,000.00 in silver quarters, or for a few twenty dollar gold pieces. These are the types of trades that you'll be able to take advantage of if you've properly positioned yourself. Now, if you're like everybody else in stocks and bonds, you'll be trying to get out with what's left of your skin. Take a portion of your wealth, and move it over to what the Constitution says is money, and that's gold or silver coin.

Is there practical advice for riding out a financial collapse?

People should have plenty of water and food stored in their pantry for use during periods of economic turbulence. If you have grown children not living at home, you'd be wise to also store some for them, because what happens in tough economic times is that the offspring come running back home. You may have stored enough supplies for yourself and your spouse, but that won't be enough when your hungry daughter, son-in-law, and grandchildren unexpectedly arrive at your front door. You don't want to have to try to find food on store shelves, or try to develop a barter network after the financial crisis begins. That's like attempting to purchase fire insurance with flames licking at your heels. I recently witnessed a blizzard here on the East

Coast. Over three feet of snow fell, and people were knocking each other down in the grocery store trying to get food off the shelves. I thought to myself, "this is just a little snowstorm. What is going to happen in a real economic emergency?"

How bad could things get during a total economic collapse?

The 1992 riots in Los Angeles might be considered tame compared to what could happen in US cities. Rampant arson, robbery, theft, looting, vandalism and worse should be expected. It would be survival of the fittest. That's all the more reason not to have to venture outside of your house to get a loaf of bread or milk or currency or method of exchange. You'd be better off to take these steps in advance. Stockpile a little food to feed your family, some tangible assets, and emergency water.

Who would be the biggest losers in the event of a US default?

The Federal Reserve Bank. This private bank holds the assets of the United States in the form of bonds, and for this reason they will do everything possible to prevent default.

Is gold a better investment than silver?

In short, the answer is yes - but let me explain. The photographic industry was the biggest user of silver, but they have moved over to electronic computer imaging. As a result, the industrial demand for silver has decreased substantially. In early 1993, silver was trading as low as $3.70 per ounce. But now it has risen back to the $5.50 per ounce range, based on monetary needs. I would suggest that with its traditional 15 to 1 ratio to gold, silver is a better investment, in terms of potential. But if the choice is whether to buy silver or gold, you really cannot make a bad choice. However, when it's all said and done, silver may have outperformed gold percentage-wise.

Will precious metal values rise in the near future?

I see all the metals taking a jump, as will all the commodities.

We'll see rises in commodities prices in general. Everything will be done to try to beat prices back down. We might see some horizontal movement, but generally the trend is up. Inflation is coming back, and it's coming back with a vengeance.

When is the best time to move into precious metal?

Look for a quick rise in interest rates not driven by the Fed, when the long bond takes a severe beating in price, and, consequently, a sharp rise in yield. When you see the long bond shoot up in a dramatic fashion, (having tested its bottom and then bounced off), that's your indicator that interest rates have stopped going down and will start going up. You can look for these signs, but we're on a steadily upward course now. Every tangible is starting to march straight up. The momentum is there, the psychology is there - I would just watch for that slow, steady price increase in gold. When gold breaks 450 per ounce, you won't need any more confirmation. At that point, it's "off to the races".

What does it mean when stock prices and gold prices rise at the same time?

This proves to me that it's not a healthy market. If in fact the stock market was rising, and bond market interest rates were falling for legitimate reasons, then gold would be beaten down to its all time low. But if in fact we're at a fifteen-year low on bonds, then gold should be selling for relatively nothing. They should be throwing it out of windows! But they're not. Why? Because the fuel in the stock and bond markets is not the result of a healthy economy, but rather the result of excess government funding. The Treasury Secretary has taken money which is not supposed to be circulating, money which is supposed to be sitting aside in pension funds, and he's circulating it to pay the Debt. This is precisely what has fueled the recent rise. When one examines the increases in the supply of real money, it's been remarkable. That's what really fuels inflation. Remember, that's all that inflation is. An increase in the supply of money.

What was the original function of the "derivatives market"?

If a farmer wants to plant corn, but he isn't certain what the corn will be worth at the end of the growing season, he can sell it at a fixed price before he grows it, using the derivatives market. That was the original function and proper use of the derivatives market.

Is jewelry a good investment?

I don't recommend gemstones, but 14 and 18 karat gold and sterling silver jewelry are very portable, very liquid, and are also beyond the realm of reporting requirements, for those concerned about the privacy issue.

What happens to money markets and CD's in the event of a default?

Those investors would be in last place. In first place would be Government bondholders. Individual commercial banks who are holding bonds as an asset, if they're strong enough, may get a chance to pay their depositors. The depositors are the last ones to get their money. If you have a commercial bank CD or a money market fund, you'll be last in line to get your money.

What would happen in the stock market during a default?

Stocks are an equity position. During a crash or default, the company you hold stock in could go bankrupt, or could easily multiply its wealth even while the bond market is collapsing. Money Market funds are more tied to the bond market than they are to stocks. Certain technology stocks will "clean up" in the years to come. They represent cutting-edge technologies. Also, the DOW 30s, those blue chip industrial companies, have solid asset bases. The majority have real estate that will carry the load. Therefore, I wouldn't be too worried, but, at the same time, there could be a loss of principal, even in the strongest of stocks.

Should I exchange my dollars for foreign currencies?

Not unless you plan to move to those nations to live. All the benefits of currency exchange values can be altered by government edict.

Is the Yen considered a strong currency?

I don't like the Yen. The banks in Japan hold all of their reserves in US dollars. The banking crisis in Japan is going to make our S & L crisis look like a picnic. They have real problems over there. The Yen is a puppet of the Dollar. The Japanese Central Bank and the Japanese commercial banks hold a majority of their reserves in U.S. Dollars and U.S. Treasury Bonds. In 1985 we were looking at 240 yen to the dollar. As of the first quarter, 1996 we're around 107 Yen to the Dollar. The G-7 met at the Plaza Hotel in New York, and they decided amongst themselves that they were going to let the Dollar fall to about 110 (Yen to the Dollar). Wouldn't you like to have been a fly on that wall? Can you imagine the inside information that left that room? Certainly, fortunes were made.

Can the "average investor" effectively use the derivatives market?

My problem with the derivatives market is that it's an amplification of the problem. When a boom comes (or when a bust comes) it is amplified by the derivative market. Buying contracts into the future is a risky proposition for the average investor. He could just as easily lose all his money as make any money. I prefer the physical possession market. If you're going to buy gold, then buy it; hold it in your hands and store it yourself. There won't be any margin calls, and the worst thing that can happen is that if the price of gold doesn't rise, at least you're holding an asset. If you buy an option to buy gold in the future, and the price doesn't move, every bit of money that you put up as premium is gone. While it could multiply your returns, it could certainly exaggerate your losses, and that's the main reason I don't like derivatives for the average investor.

How does today's stock market compare to the market during the so-called "Roaring Twenties"?

The 1920s were termed "roaring" because of the presence of all the "hot" money that was initially created to finance World War One. As it filtered back from Europe into the US during the 20's, this "war money" poured into the stock market, nudging prices higher and higher and pushing real estate values to unheard-of levels. Ultimately that inflation was followed by a collapse called the Great Depression. Within the coming years there will be drastic monetary shifts in the US economy, and the people who currently have piles of Federal Reserve notes or large investments denominated in Federal Reserve Notes are the people who will suffer the most. The average wage earner will not be hit very hard. Debtors will do best of all, because they will be able to pay off loans with dollars worth much less than those borrowed.

Will the debit card eventually give way to an encoded data chip which will be implanted under the skin?

The technology is certainly there. By the time such a scenario occurs, if it occurs, our society will have already turned into a cashless one, with most transactions occurring electronically, and this chip might be offered as a "convenience".

Will the Government ever confiscate Krugerrands?

They may, as they did in the 1930's under the authority of the Gold Hoarding Act. There are two risks or potential problems with Krugerrands. IRS Section 6045-B basically says that if you sell your Krugerrands, your Social Security number must be recorded and reported to the Treasury. The other potential problem is created by the Trading with the Enemy Act of 1917, as amended in 1934, which says that the President, at his discretion, can outlaw the private ownership of gold bullion, which includes Krugerrands and other bullion coins. I would urge you to trade your Krugerrands for old, circulated 20 dollar gold pieces, or even low-grade uncirculated 20 dollar gold pieces. If a Krugerrand sells for $425, you can expect to pay $500 for a 20 dollar gold coin in well-circulated condition. For that little bit of difference, you would be well-advised to purchase the US coin, where you'd have insurance against possible confiscation.

Do you recommend municipal bonds as an investment vehicle?

No. Unlike stocks, bonds are all tied together with one rope. The minute that the Treasury bond yield falls, that's it - it's over. All the municipal and corporate bonds go down right along with it. In the stock market, one stock can completely collapse and the others can continue. If there is any "break" in the price of Treasury bonds, it will drag all brands of commercial paper right down the tubes with it. You're looking at six percent yield "long rates". If inflation is three or four percent, what is your actual net gain?

Should I keep some "rainy-day cash" in my shoe box?

If you're "storing" a lot of cash you have a problem. The currency changeover is really an attempt to flush out the underground economy. Many people have been storing unreported cash over the years. The money changeover will catch a great deal of that. If you have that much cash, get out of it. Keeping cash in the mattress is like keeping your milk on the porch. It's spoiling while you're holding it. You'd be much better off to buy food; to buy gold and silver coins; to buy art, antiques, an old automobile, or even an old Harley Davidson motorcycle. I can think of a hundred alternatives which are better than keeping your wealth stored in cash.

Should I make a special effort to pay off existing mortgages, so that I own all real estate free and clear?

If you have a fixed mortgage, or an adjustable rate mortgage capped under 10 percent, rather than attempting to double up on your mortgage payments, you would be well advised to put excess cash into gold or silver. Certainly I would consider the equity I had in the house. The notion of having your house paid for "free and clear" is a outdated one. Your house will not go up any faster or slower if you have a big mortgage or a small mortgage. It doesn't make much sense to leave all your equity locked up in an asset that could disappear. What are you going to do if interest rates go to fourteen percent? Are you going to then try to borrow the money out of your house? You're much better off to take care of it when interest rates are low. If you have a lot of equity built up, take some of it now and put it into a tangible asset. Instead of doubling the mortgage payments, pick up some survival silver or gold coins which will protect you better than an extra mortgage payment.

What is the best general investment advice?

Acquire tangibles.   Invest in anything but debt.   Don't denominate your wealth in debt. That's the best advice. Look at whatever you call an asset, and if it represents debt, get rid of it. Get on the equity side of the journal, preferably a physical possession equity... something that you can hold in your hand.

Are credit unions the same thing as banks?

Credit unions, generally speaking, don't "create" money. That's the primary difference. They take a deposit from you, and they loan it to someone else. I like credit unions because it's honest banking. Commercial banks create money out of thin air, so they have an advantage over credit unions. I would suggest that if you have money in a credit union, you've got to understand that it's tied to your neighbor's 30-year mortgage. If you don't mind having money in there for 30 years, it's a great place to put it. If you're looking for a short-term out, you might get caught in a squeeze if a bunch of depositors start requesting their money back, and the Credit Union has it all loaned out in 30-year mortgages.

What is your long-range forecast for our economy?

I foresee a slow, steady inflationary cycle that will eventually wipe out the purchasing power of today's dollar. But it will be done at such a slow, steady and insidious pace that not one man in a million will realize what's going on. They'll just wake up 10 or 15 years down the road and realize how much more expensive things are.

What happens if investors and institutions around the world lose faith in the US Government's ability to pay its obligations, and stop purchasing US Treasury Bonds?

Under normal circumstances, the Government can create debt, and then move a portion of this debt into the future by selling Treasury Bonds to the citizens. It's borrowing from the future because eventually that debt must be repaid. When uncertainty exists, people flock to cash. They convert all of their long-term debt into liquid cash, and that reduces the immediate purchasing power of the represented dollar. Every attempt is made to reverse this trend, such as Nixon's Wage and Price controls, or President Roosevelt's gold seizure. But if the people can't be persuaded to put their money back into long term debt, then the Federal Reserve is forced to "monetize" this debt, and either print the money or default. Of course, the only politically sound policy is to create more money. This means the devaluation of all existing Federal Reserve Notes. This is how the Federal Government will repay the Federal Debt. They will pay it with dollars worth substantially less than the dollars that they borrowed in the first place.

Are we moving into a completely cashless society?

An electronic currency is the single biggest threat to our financial independence. In 1933, our bankers had a problem: they held a supply of gold that was "X", and they had a supply of notes that was "2X". Their solution was to prevent American citizens from redeeming their notes for gold. Now we fast forward to the present. Our paper money supply is less than 500 billion dollars. But the total money supply is five trillion dollars. What does that mean? If just 10 percent of the "money" was withdrawn in cash tomorrow, there wouldn't be enough. So the solution to this problem, from the banking industry's perspective, is to eliminate cash. If Americans don't use cash, then all of the money stays within a closed system and can be monitored and controlled. A controlled inflation is relatively easy to swallow. Five or six percent per year inflation is tolerable. Even though we lose 50 percent of our purchasing power every few years, we won't complain. Many experts are contemplating with trepidation an economic future containing a total monetary meltdown, with complete chaos and ruin. But actually we shouldn't worry about a total collapse with the world "coming to an end". Conversion to electronic currency, and a steady, controlled inflation of eight to ten percent annually is what we should be preparing for. There are some financial maneuvers being planned for us that will not be good for the average American.

What will the economic landscape look like twenty years from now?

I don't see anything vaguely resembling a "Mad Max" post-apocalyptic economy. Rather, we'll be sitting in our rocking chairs talking about how we would work all day for one hundred dollars, and our children will be rolling on the ground, laughing at us, because they wouldn't even bend over to pick up a one hundred dollar bill off the floor!

What will the tax rates be twenty years from now?

Bill Clinton's own 1996 budget predicted that the next generation will be paying 82 percent of its life-time earnings in taxes.

Is there a simple formula for restoring the economy?

When you grow vegetables out of the ground, you are producing real wealth. When you exchange paper dollars for produce, you are not producing anything. That's what we need to get back to in this country, a production-based economy. We need to base taxation on consumption and untax America's production. If we would just take those steps and remonetize our Federal Reserve System with United States Notes, we could have this Republic back on a steady course within five years.

What will happen to the mortgage interest rate deduction?

Nothing. It's a sacred cow. There are too many lobbyists and they're much too strong.

What will the economic landscape look like as we enter the 21st Century?

We can expect a re-run of 1977 to 1980. A slow, steady inflationary cycle will result in double-digit interest rates, double-digit inflation, and skyrocketing commodities prices.

Can America ever get its financial house in order?

It's doubtful. If the present trends continue, we're looking at a seven to eight trillion dollar debt by the time we actually start paying principal. With that, we're talking 500 to 700 billion dollars annual interest. I think it's impossible to get a handle on our financial situation unless we get a handle on the way it's financed.

Historically, what has happened to those nations who do not get their financial houses in order?

It always ends in one of two options. Either an outright public declaration of bankruptcy, or default. Option two is a hyper-inflation similar to post World War One Germany, where it took a wheel barrow filled with money to buy a loaf of bread. These are the only two options. Make no mistake. Every unbacked currency in the history of the world has collapsed. Every one, with not a single exception.

Why are rare coins considered to be a safer investment vehicle than gold bullion?

In the past, governments have, when it suited their purposes, confiscated gold and silver from private owners, and then quickly placed those confiscated metals back onto the market at increased prices. Indeed, while precious metal bullion exists as a valid vehicle for the protection of wealth, it has been stolen from the people many times in the past. Coins which are considered to have "collectible value" have been excluded from previous confiscation orders. The reason for this is that the international rich have invested their own wealth in gold and silver coins. Coins of collector value are specifically exempt from confiscation, per the 1933 Gold Hoarding Act.

What is "junk silver"?

These are pre-1965 dimes, quarters, and half-dollars which can be used for spending money in the event of a hyperinflation.

When is a good time to enter the coin market?

Every market is cyclical. When interest rates are climbing, inflation fears are rising, and monetary crises are looming, that is the time when investment grade US gold and silver coins outperform every other investment in the marketplace. In the period from 1977 to 80, the average rare coin went up almost 1000 percent. It's when interest rates are low and inflation is perceived not to be a problem that investors should move into these types of tangibles.

How do investors know they are getting a good value when they purchase a rare coin?

I speak to many wealthy investors on a daily basis who consider themselves well-diversified. But all of their assets have one thing in common. They are all paper or dollar-denominated investments. They don't really know that the rare coin market offers an alternative to paper investments. The best thing I can recommend to these investors is to first educate themselves. The US Postal Service has published an informative booklet on coin collecting in co-operation with the Federal Trade Commission. I also publish several free booklets. Get them and read them. Determine for yourself where the market lies, where the liquidity is, and then move some of your assets in that area. Educating oneself about the coin market is a simple thing to do.

Can gold coins outperform the gold market?

The factors that cause gold to rise in value are the same factors that produce a rise in the gold coin market. But there is an important additional factor with gold coin investments. As investors flock into a limited supply market such as twenty dollar gold pieces, they get an extra premium. When gold went from 103 to 850 dollars per ounce, a Krugerrand, containing one ounce of gold, also went from 103 to 850 dollars per ounce, but a one ounce twenty dollar gold piece went from 105 dollars to 2,500 dollars. Because there are only so many twenty dollar gold pieces available, that extra "supply and demand factor" created a huge dividend for the gold coin investor. As investors chase a limited number of coins, the price rises. The same ratios are true as the price of gold falls. That coin that rose to 2,500 dollars has fallen all the way back to 600 dollars.

How does an investor know when to jump into the coin market, and how does one know when to jump back out?

If you bought coins in 1980 <u>after</u> interest rates had already risen for a period of three years (with inflation on everyone's mind), and sold them today, you would be losing over half of your investment. Clearly, timing is critical. Generally, when interest rates are low and have been falling for a sustained period of time, the time to buy coins has arrived. When interest rates are high, and have been rising for a sustained period of time, that's when you sell coins. If you follow that rule of thumb, you can time market cycles in seven to ten year swings, and not have that overnight worry which many investors have.

Who is the "typical" rare-coin investor?

It's not the person who needs his paycheck dollars for short term solutions. If you're a person who has stocks and bonds, owns his home, and it's not going to change your lifestyle to take five or ten percent of your assets and move into this area, then it's perfect for you. One of the things required are "strong hands". You have to plan to hold something at least five to seven years. If you're in the short-term market, and wish to keep your money very liquid for use next year, then coins are not for you.

What percentage of an investor's portfolio should be allocated to rare coin purchases?

Most prudent financial planners will recommend ten percent of an investment portfolio in a tangible. I have clients who have as much as one-half of their investment dollars shifted over into the tangibles market. If you think that the dollar is somehow going to stop its eighty-year slide, then turn around and start gaining value, and if you're certain that the Government is going to get its house in order the way they promised in Gramm-Rudman, then you probably don't want to buy coins. But if you think it's going to be more "business as usual" - more debt, more inflation - then coins are certainly the vehicle in which to place more than ten percent of your investment dollars.

What specific coins should investors seek?

It depends on the size of the investment. One man's ceiling is another man's floor. When Kidder Peabody decided that it was going to invest fifteen million dollars in the coin market, it didn't go out and buy five-thousand-dollar coins. It went out and bought million-dollar coins. The same should be true of the individual investor. First, determine the size of your total investment, then make it so that ten percent of your coin dollars are not tied up in any one coin. If you do that, then you'll enjoy success. Diversification is the key in the coin market.

How do coins compare to cash as far as privacy is concerned?

To ensure privacy, many individuals store their cash in safe deposit boxes, in shoe boxes, and even under the proverbial mattress. Storing cash under your mattress is like putting an uncashed check under your mattress. Anything can happen to it in the interim, because it is not real wealth. It is a representation of wealth. My grandfather would work a week for a twenty dollar gold piece, and most people today would work a week for a twenty dollar gold piece. If you are going to store your wealth privately for the long term, there is no better vehicle than United States Coins. Even when gold was illegal to own, you could sell a twenty dollar gold piece to the Attorney General of the United States and be within the law. It is the best privacy and financial insurance vehicle available. I think that not enough people take advantage of it. With a twenty dollar gold piece you have anonymity, you can buy and sell without a Social Security Number, you can pass it on as twenty-dollars to your children, and you could pay your taxes with it if you were so inclined.

Why should US coins be part of every investor's portfolio?

With the National debt surging past the five-trillion-dollar figure, and a projected debt of eight-trillion dollars by the end of the decade, our government is faced with only two options. It can either inflate the money supply and pay it off, or it can default. Either scenario is good for coins. We've come through a market period of falling interest rates. All markets are cyclical. As interest rates rise again, investors will enjoy the rewards that were experienced by those in the gold and coin markets during the period of 1977 to 1980. Timing is the issue, and clearly now is the time to move into the coin market. As money changes form and becomes electronic, the desire to own real money will become ever stronger. On to the 21st Century!